MATCH OF
MY LIFE

From one St Mary's
boy to another!
All the best Gerard

from

John

THE HEAVY WOOLLEN VICTORIES

1973 ▮ 2010

JOHN ROE

Scratching Shed Publishing Ltd

Typeset in Warnock Pro Semi Bold and Palatino
Printed and bound in the United Kingdom by

Short Run Press Ltd
Bittern Road, Sowton Industrial Estate, Exeter. EX2 7LW
Tel: 01392 211909   Fax: 01392 444134

For my late father (an ardent Batley fan) who, in 1973, said:
'Yeah, I suppose that Mick Stephenson can play a bit'.
And – had he been alive in 2010 – would undoubtedly have said:
'A decent enough performance;
nob'dy going bloody bomb happy and nob'dy tubbing it.'
Also, for all my 'Looking Back' friends: Allison, Martin, Mel,
Keith, Michael, Neil, Paul, Ron, Richard and Brian.

Also by this author

Sermons from the Mount – Recollections of Batley RLFC

From the Mountaintop – An Archive of Batley RLFC
(With Terry Swift, Ken Pearson and Craig Lingard)

Contents

Foreword

✳ Craig Lingard ✳

RUGBY LEAGUE HERITAGE in the Heavy Woollen District has somehow become a huge part of the life of someone who originates from Wakefield.

The journey, for me, started when I signed for Batley Bulldogs in 1998, aged 19. I was fortunate enough not only to represent the club over 200 times, but also to become the club's all-time record try scorer which, although it was a huge personal achievement, didn't really impact on me emotionally until many years later.

This happened when I took on the responsibility – along with a very dedicated band of volunteers – of researching the history of Batley RLFC. This project was initially meant to last three years, but due to the onset of Covid it became part of my life for nearly five. During that time I immersed myself in the club's story, particularly its early years, and read innumerable newspaper articles and stories about huge successes and even bigger struggles; details of its famous players and some that only played a handful of games; the part the Bulldogs – and formerly Gallant Youths – played in the community; and how important the club is to the Heavy Woollen District.

The Heavy Woollen Victories

Seeing my own name associated with such talents as Wattie Peers Davies, Joe Oakland, Ted Fozzard, John B Goodall, Ike Fowler, Frank Gallagher, John Etty, Harold V Nunn, George Brown, Bill Riches and many, many more was when it really hit home how much it meant to be record try-scorer at Mount Pleasant.

I already knew, of course, that my dad, Steve, had played for Batley in the 1970s, but through our research also discovered that one of my grandads and two of his brothers also represented the club. Without me knowing it, the Lingard family and Batley RL already had a connection many years before I signed 25 years ago.

At the commencement of the 2023 season, 1,757 players had worn the Batley colours and I am proud and honoured to have been one of them. Furthemore, I have also had the privilege of being an assistant coach and head coach, and so pleased that this kid from Wakefield took the gamble to go for a trial at Batley Bulldogs.

Craig Lingard

Introduction

* John Roe *

BATLEY AND DEWSBURY are the professional rugby league clubs whose two grounds are in closest proximity to each other, roughly a couple of miles apart. In fact, Dewsbury's stadium is located only just beyond Batley's official boundary. Both towns are part of West Yorkshire's Heavy Woollen District, though little of the industrial activity which gave the region its name now remains.

These clubs, having emerged in the 19th century partly as a manifestation of thriving economic activity and civic pride, have a rich heritage.

Batley, whose 'Rugby' side was added to the existing Cricket and Athletic Club in 1880, was among the Northern Union's founder members in 1895, the organisation subsequently rebranded as 'The Rugby League'. As inaugural winners of the Challenge Cup in 1897, retaining it in 1898 before winning it for a third time in 1901, all three games at Headingley, Batley are still the only team to contest three or more Challenge Cup finals without defeat. Moreover, their ground at Mount Pleasant holds the record for the longest history of professional rugby league being played on a site in the world.

Dewsbury, established in 1875, are an older club yet missed out on founder-member status by delaying their entry to the Northern Union until 1897. But having first won the Cup in 1912, they have actually played in Challenge Cup final at Wembley – and not just any final either. In fact, they played in the very first one to be staged at the old Empire Stadium, losing 13-2 to Wigan before a crowd of 41,500, on Saturday 4 May 1929. In August 2023, Batley did at last walk out on the hallowed turf, but were beaten 12-10 by Halifax Panthers in the final of the lower division AB Sundecks 1895 Cup.

Batley RLFC's 'glory years' were most definitely before World War One, although the club did manage to win the Championship trophy in 1924. Dewsbury, after their first Challenge Cup win, then had to wait 31 years to win it again, when the final was played over two legs in 1943. In fact, during World War Two, a Dewsbury team put together and managed by the future BBC radio and television commentator Eddie Waring, contained many famous guest players, leading to some of the most exciting rugby their spectators had ever seen. After which, the 1950s and 1960s were, for the most part, lean years for both Heavy Woollen clubs. In the end, Batley had to wait rather longer than Dewsbury for another taste of success, the latter lifting the Championship trophy in 1973, the former winning the Northern Rail Cup in 2010.

In both instances, the final victory generally came as a surprise to commentators and spectators alike, but not necessarily to those most closely involved – the players and coaches. It is undoubtedly true that neither Dewsbury in 1973 nor Batley in 2010 were obvious favourites to win either game, but closer analysis, as will be shown, reveals that their ultimate victories were not as surprising as they may at first have seemed. There are also marked similarities between the events, although Dewsbury's was the greater achievement in so far as it occurred within a competition that included all the Rugby League's professional clubs (even allowing for how it occurred in the pre-Super League era) while, as with the 1895 Cup, the Northern Rail Cup competition excluded teams from Super League.

In the first instance, it should be noted that both Dewsbury's team in 1973 and Batley's in 2010 was made up of players drawn from the immediate or near locality and contained a blend of young and more experienced players. Their subsequent cohesive nature owed much to them being held together by a powerful team spirit.

Similarly, at the heart of both was a commitment to resolute defence, a feature also particularly prominent during Dewsbury's Championship semi-final victory over Warrington and Batley's Northern Rail Cup semi-final win against Leigh, matches which the Heavy Woollen clubs' opponents were strongly fancied to win.

Finally, both Dewsbury in 1973 and Batley in 2010 were guided by inspirational coaches. Although in many ways different from each other, Tommy Smales and Karl Harrison were vital components of the winning formulae, their attitude to defence an aspect of the two victories discernable in their longer-term impact on the clubs.

Looking back today, however, Batley's Northern Rail Cup win appears to have provided a platform for sustained success rather more than did Dewsbury's stunning Championship victory.

While interviewing the players, coaches and fans of both teams for this book, I was struck by the extent to which their recollection of events recounted reignited in them the sheer passion, excitement and joy of what they had experienced.

For the now former-players in particular, the memories evoked helped them to reinforce the extent and importance of what they had achieved for themselves, their club and community.

It was a delight and a privilege to record all of these memories, recollections interwoven with the author's own observations along with contemporary reports in the press.

John Roe
January 2024

PART 1

DEWSBURY RLFC 1973 – RUGBY LEAGUE CHAMPIONS

1.

THE ROAD TO THE CHAMPIONSHIP FINAL

THE DEWSBURY TEAM *that beat Leeds 22-13 in the Rugby League Championship final at Odsal Stadium on Saturday 19 May 1973 was: Adrian Rushton, Greg Ashcroft, John Clark, Nigel Stephenson, Terry Day, Allan Agar, Alan Bates, Harry Beverley, Mick Stephenson, Trevor Lowe, Jeff Grayshon, John Bates, Joe Whittington.*
Substitutes: Steve Lee, Brian Taylor.

Apart from Greg Ashcroft, who was from Wales, the players were from West Yorkshire, from the Dewsbury, Batley, Featherstone and Wakefield region. It was a team from the local area.

Tommy Smales

What was great was that so many of the lads were local. Me, Mick Stephenson, Alan Bates, John Bates and Joe Whittington were from Dewsbury. John Clark was from Batley and Jeff Grayshon was from Birstall.

Nigel Stephenson

One of the great things about that team is that they were local lads. They weren't all from Dewsbury, but the ones who weren't were mainly from nearby. A few had played at Shaw Cross, an amateur club which doesn't get the recognition it deserves. Jeff Grayshon didn't play junior rugby and initially signed as a fullback or centre. Tommy Smales switched him to the second row for a game against Halifax and he was man of the match. A phenomenal decision.

Geoff Berry (lifelong fan and former referee)

Geoff alludes to the fact that some members of the Dewsbury team had relatively little experience of playing rugby league before they signed for the club, a fact borne out by the testimony of Jeff Grayshon and John Bates:

From Dawson's to Dewsbury

I started off working at Dawson's in Gomersal as an apprentice pipe fitter and got to play for the firm's team on a Sunday morning in a work's competition. We got to the final, but we lost.

In the meantime, a local scout who had links with Dewsbury asked me to go for trials. I had five or six games and then they wanted to sign me. I got £100 and was over the moon with that because my wage at the time, since I was only an apprentice, was £3 odd a week. When I got the cheque, I was dancing. I might have been able to get more, but I was never greedy about money.

Jeff Grayshon

We just rang the Chairman

I never played for an amateur team. I went to Earlsheaton secondary school and they didn't play rugby there. Me and my brother, Alan, used to play on the fields doing proper tackling, but we never went to play for Shaw Cross even though it was close by. My dad didn't want us to join Shaw Cross. I'm not sure why.

Trevor Mitchell suggested that we should ring up Dewsbury and ask if we could get a trial. So we rang the chairman, Brearley Bailey, from a phone box and he was a bit hesitant but said we could come along. We were still teenagers, about seventeen or eighteen. Alan is a year younger than me. Three of us went for a trial. There was me, Alan and Trevor Mitchell, whose idea it was, and in the end he was the only one who wasn't signed on.

I was a bit worried that they might not want Alan because he was too small. He was stocky and as hard as nails, but not very tall. I got fifty pounds for signing on, though Alan didn't get anything at first but he stuck out for a fee. I said he had to, because he owed me £25!

I suppose it was quite unusual to be signed on without having played for a recognised amateur team.

John Bates

Although Jeff, John and Alan lacked an amateur pedigree, they both went on to gain international honours. However, they were the exceptions as most members of the team had risen through the amateur ranks at local clubs like Shaw Cross and Thornhill.

A good amateur apprenticeship

I signed for Dewsbury in 1968 at the same time as a number of other players. I had played for Shaw Cross Boys from being 15 years old. We were very well coached there; they showed us how to tackle and pass the ball properly.

John Clark

In 1973, the vast majority of the Dewsbury squad was relatively unknown, especially by comparison with the Leeds team with whom they contested the Championship final.

It is true that Nigel Stephenson, Alan Bates, Harry Beverley, Jeff Grayshon and John Bates subsequently represented their country, but Mick Stephenson, who had already played at international level, was the only well-known member of the Dewsbury team at the time.

Needless to say, Mick, who later morphed into the Sky TV presenter Mike 'Stevo' Stephenson, was the undoubted star player of the team; a colourful character and an inspiration to others.

Self-styled 'sanitary inspector' and star player

I worked at Beaumont and Blackburn's in Dewsbury, as a plumber. I'd started on the painting and decorating side but kept getting a rash from the lead in the paint, so they switched me to plumbing. Even though it was nearly all lead piping I didn't have the same reaction because it was the lead mixing with some chemical in the paint that was causing the problem.

Mike 'Stevo' Stephenson

Stevo said that he was a sanitary inspector, but he was a plumber. He was always out and about round Dewsbury talking to people. It's no surprise that he became such a great commentator on Sky.

He was a fantastic player was Mick. He had a lovely burst of speed over about thirty yards. I can remember in one game he emerged from a competitive scrum and somehow he was backing up a player, took the pass and scored under the posts. I wasn't the quickest player, but I don't know how he got there ahead of me!

He was a great player who had lovely hands and he could also kick goals. There wasn't much he couldn't do on a rugby field. He used to act as a sort of sweeper behind the main line of tacklers, so if someone broke through Stevo was there to tackle them. Normally he didn't have to do many tackles in a match because they didn't get through the first line. He was a great talker and he loved talking, organising the players on the field and he could make sure that we stuck to Tommy's plan.

Nigel Stephenson

The 'outsider' in the Dewsbury team was Welsh winger, Greg Ashcroft, now sadly deceased. Greg, as his widow Diane explains below, was a talented athlete.

Athletics, basketball and rugby

Greg had played rugby union for the Welsh youth team and for Pontypridd. He moved to Dewsbury to play rugby league, but his first love was athletics. He was in the British youth team as a sprinter and held the Welsh youth record for the hundred yards. I think it's still unbroken. He loved sprinting, won the Pontypridd Taff Street Dash several times. He raced against Welsh rugby union winger J J Williams, who also died quite recently, two months after Greg.

Greg played basketball for the Welsh youth team. He just loved sport. He was the 'Welsh Youth Sportsman of the Year' as a teenager.

Diane Ashcroft (Greg Ashcroft's widow)

Whilst Dewsbury's victory on 19th July 1973 was the crowning glory of their season, the team might have enjoyed even more spectacular success.

What might have been

We could have won three trophies that year. We lost to Leeds in the Yorkshire Cup final (me and Nigel Stephenson used to joke that we lost because me and Nigel didn't play) and then lost to Bradford in the Challenge Cup semi-final at Headingley. We never performed on the day and when we came off the field I just said to Jeff Grayshon "We just weren't good enough." After that, though, we never lost a match and that was great preparation for that Championship final.

Joe Whittington

THE PLAY-OFFS

At the end of the 1972/73 season, Dewsbury had finished in eighth position in the league, which meant that it was likely that only their first fixture in the play-offs for the Championship trophy would be a guaranteed home game.

If they were going to win the trophy, they were going to have to do it the hard way. They faced Oldham, who had finished one place below them, in the first round and then they had to travel mid-week to Featherstone, who had finished second in the table and were shortly to play in the Challenge Cup final against Bradford Northern.

Two comfortable victories, even against Frank Foster

In the run-up to the final, from the first play-off game against Oldham things happened very quickly. It was the top 16 teams that were involved in the play-offs and we finished in 8th place, so we played at home against Oldham, who had finished 9th, in the first play-off match, which we won easily.

Then we played mid-week at Featherstone, who had finished 2nd in the league, and hammered them, 26-7.

Peter Fox slipped up by resting two international players in the first half. By the time they came on in the second half, we were too far ahead.

Tommy Smales

We beat Oldham at Crown Flatt in the first round but then we had to play teams that had finished much higher up the table.

After Oldham we played Featherstone away and Peter Fox was their coach. They went to Wembley soon after and beat Bradford Northern to win the Challenge Cup, as well as finishing second in the table.

Peter decided to give Nash and Bridges, two internationals, a rest by making them substitutes. Featherstone were losing by 16 points to nil after a quarter of an hour, so Fox decided it was time for them to come on, but he took them off again later. We beat Featherstone comfortably and some years later when I worked at the same place as Peter Fox, I asked him why he had taken Nash and Bridges off and he told me that it was because he had a soft spot for Dewsbury!

Nigel Stephenson

We played Oldham first in the top 16 play-offs and I actually scored a try in that match. Frank Foster was playing for Oldham, so I was up against him. What a brute, he used to frighten players to death. Anyway, he actually complimented me at the end of the game.

Once when I played against him, I hit him with a tackle in the chest and he fell back in the mud. I thought, if he gets up he'll kill me, so I put some distance between us.

After Oldham, our play-off games were away. We played at Featherstone mid-week and they thought it would be no contest, but we beat them comfortably even though it was a tough game.

Joe Whittington

Allan Agar is from Featherstone and had been at the club before he moved on to play for Dewsbury. Consequently, when Dewsbury comfortably beat Featherstone in the second round of the play-offs, he was the obvious target for the anger and frustration of his home town supporters.

I couldn't get out of the ground

On the way to the final we beat Featherstone at Post Office Road and I couldn't get out of the ground I was getting that much stick.

Featherstone were in the Challenge Cup final and they didn't think that we would beat them. I worked at Yorkshire Copper Works in Leeds and Peter Fox, the Featherstone coach, worked there as well. He rang me up to try to find out how individual players were playing, hoping to get some advantage. Anyway, it didn't work.

Nobody thought that we had a chance against Featherstone and this might have rubbed off on some of their team.

Allan Agar

An outstanding try

We finished 8th in the league so played Oldham, who had finished 16th, and that was the only home game we played. There wasn't any expectation that we could win the Championship, but we just kept on improving.

We wouldn't normally have expected to beat Featherstone away because they had a strong side and had reached the Challenge Cup final, but I remember Greg Ashcroft scoring an outstanding try from quite a way out. He was very fast. He only needed an inch and he was away.

John Bates

The Heavy Woollen Victories

'Stevo' used his pace

We had a fairly easy victory against Oldham in the first round of the play-offs and then had to go to Featherstone and play a mid-week game against them. They were going to be at Wembley in about ten days time, so they were a good team, but we beat them comfortably even though they had finished higher up the league than us

I can remember Mick Stephenson going round Cyril Kellett, the Featherstone fullback, to score a try. He just outpaced him.

John Clark

A fan's low expectations

I went to all the play-off matches. When we played the first game, against Oldham, we had just lost the Challenge Cup semi-final to Bradford, so I thought that the players would be downhearted and I didn't have very high expectations because they had missed their opportunity to play at Wembley.

I was surprised and very pleased by their performance, then when we went to Featherstone I wasn't particularly confident that we'd win, but we turned them over. The players were really buzzing and seemed to have developed the confidence that they could.

Geoff Berry

The Press and the early rounds of the play-offs

As might be expected, the local newspaper, The Dewsbury Reporter, from the outset took a keen interest in Dewsbury's progress through the play-offs. In his report of the match against Oldham, in the 4th May 1973 edition, reporter R Stansfield describes their performance as one which combined teamwork interspersed with individual skill and brilliance, highlighting the particular contributions of Jeff Grayshon and John Bates.

In the following quote, Stansfield responds to a suggestion Nigel Stephenson is slow and selfish: 'Three minutes into the second half he sprinted into a gap, swerved past deputy fullback Davies and when he

could have scored himself, gave Mick Stephenson the pass to go under the posts for his 50th try in first team football. Nigel added the goal to put Dewsbury 17-9 ahead and gave his colleagues scope to start putting on the agony, putting on the style.'

In the same edition, Stansfield begins his report of Dewsbury's defeat of Featherstone with 'How about that then?' According to him... 'Dewsbury trampled on Featherstone's double hopes to reach their first Championship semi-final after a confident, cool and classy display.'

Warming to his subject, Stansfield refers to a 'Harlem Globetrotters' set move in which a player took a pass at right angles and cites this as a prime example of the way in which individuals take second place to the team as a whole.

The Yorkshire Post, 2nd May, 1973, in a report by Alfred Drewry under the heading 'Featherstone Pay the Price', also covered Dewsbury's victory at Post Office Road. Drewry points out that Featherstone rested six of their players in preparation for their upcoming Challenge Cup Final game against Bradford – Nash, Bridges and Thompson amongst them. Nash and Bridges came on in the second half, but by then it was too late to repair the damage. This may have reflected a degree of complacency on the part of the Featherstone coach, Peter Fox, or it may be that he was simply prioritising what was then the more prestigious trophy, the Challenge Cup.

According to Drewry, Dewsbury got better and better as the game progressed. Interestingly, Mick Stephenson, not known for his hooking abilities, won five out of the first six scrums, whilst Dewsbury's planned moves proved too much for the Featherstone defence to cope with.

Drewry suggests that during the second half Featherstone began to accept the inevitable and that their principal aim was to ensure that their key players remained free from injury, ahead of the Challenge Cup final.

The semi-final against Warrington

Warrington had finished top of the table, so a semi-final on the 'Wire's home turf at Wilderspool was a daunting task for Dewsbury. Nonetheless, R Stansfield writing in the Dewsbury Reporter, 4th May,

*1973, under the heading 'Let 'em all come now say fearless Dewsbury',
was particularly upbeat about Dewsbury's chances of reaching the
Championship final, even going as far as describing Warrington as 'a
tough uncompromising side, but uninventive', a somewhat strange
description given that Alex Murphy was the player-coach and
inspiration of the team.*

*Michael Lumb, the Dewsbury President, claimed that Dewsbury
had, even whilst losing, secured a moral victory in their league match
at Warrington because they had fought back from being 18-7 down
at half-time to a final score of 23-19, thus winning the second half 12-
5. Obviously this was part of a strategy of boosting the team's morale
ahead of what was certainly going to be a very tough semi-final at
Warrington, Dewsbury's third match in the space of a week.*

One of the best games I witnessed as a coach

We went to Warrington three or four days after the Featherstone
game, at the weekend, and that was a really tough game because
Warrington had finished top of the table.

That was one of the best games I witnessed as a coach. We knew
that Murphy would kick to Greg Ashcroft, thinking that he would
be a weak link, so we practised kicking to Greg and it paid off.

Greg was Welsh and had come from rugby union, so he was a bit
green at first but he was eager to learn and I brought him on over
two years. In the match against Warrington he was up against their
international winger, John Bevan, and Greg held his own against
him.

It was the same with John Clark in the centre. He developed over
a couple of years. He was a very good tackler.

And there was Nigel Stephenson, the other centre, who was
brilliant; lovely footballer. Because there was such a small gap
between the game against Featherstone and the game against
Warrington, we only did light training. We concentrated on three-
quarter sprints.

Tommy Smales

A fantastic tackle

The semi-final at Warrington was a really tough game because they had Alex Murphy and some other internationals like John Bevan.

I scored a try in that match from an Alan Bates pass, but I remember a fantastic tackle by Adrian Rushton as Bevan was diving to score a try just next to the corner flag. Adrian took him out in mid-air. It was a fantastic tackle.

Adrian Rushton was one of the unsung heroes of that team. He was a great tackler and he could catch the high kicks all day long.

Nigel Stephenson

My best play-off match

The semi-final against Warrington was my best play-off match.

Before the game, me and Jeff Grayshon had a chat in the changing room about what we'd do. We knew it was going to be difficult because they had a lot of internationals in their team. At the end of the game Tommy Smales ran onto the field and lifted me up.

Alex Murphy, Warrington's player-coach, had been screaming at his team. He was gutted that day because he was never thinking that he would lose to Dewsbury. Defensively, that day we were great.

We knew that if we were ten points ahead, we would win because we could keep the other team out. At one point Warrington must have had about twelve tackles very close to our line, but they couldn't get through our defence.

Joe Whittington

A few set plays did the trick

The semi-final against Warrington was a tough game. We certainly weren't expected to win that one, so it took the pressure off us. Tommy said that we could use a few set plays to find them out and in the end we won. They were a very good team. They had Alex Murphy and Parry Gordon in the side. It was close but we managed to get through to the final.

Allan Agar

He said he hadn't done it

The game against Warrington was really hard because they had some top players: John Bevan, Dave Chisnall and Alex Murphy. I can remember Alan, who must have cracked someone, pleading with Alex Murphy that it wasn't him, that he hadn't done it.

John Bates

Murphy's strategy didn't work

It was a great win against Featherstone (26-7), especially as they went on to win the Challenge Cup, but we had to go Warrington who had Alex Murphy as their player-coach.

He could lift his team when he was on the field and I had played with him in his last international for Great Britain in 1970; he had been a hero of mine. When we tossed the coin, Alex said to me: 'I don't know why you even bothered to turn up.'

I just said: 'We'll wait and see.'

Alex said: 'Tell your Welsh winger that he's going to get plenty of practice today.' Anyway, when we had been getting changed I had told Greg Ashcroft that he was going to get peppered with high kicks. He was not the best catcher of the ball and, normally, if he caught fifty per cent of what came his way, we thought that was a bonus. Greg said to me: 'Boyo, you look to what you do.'

We didn't have much confidence that he would catch the kicks. Normally Adrian Rushton would try to get into position to take them, but in this game Greg didn't drop one.

If there was ever a game in which team spirit was the deciding factor, this was it. We were not overconfident, but we knew that if we got our defence right in the first 15 minutes, we could match them. It was a very tough game and we didn't try too many moves; just stuck at it.

Alex Murphy, I'll give him his due, came over, shook hands and said: 'I never thought you could do it.'

Mike 'Stevo' Stephenson

We kept Murphy quiet and my belief grew

The game against Warrington was a really hard one. We were worried that Alex Murphy might run the show, but we kept him quiet and stopped him from getting on top of us. I remember that we had to tackle like maniacs because they were a good team.

We were pretty exhausted by the end of the match and we all had to go to work the next day. When we beat Warrington and got through to the final, I began to think that we might be able to win because we'd beaten two really good teams to get there. We were all fit and strong and we were a fairly young team. We had a few older ones like Trevor Lowe and John Bates, but they were good players.

Jeff Grayshon

Warrington spurned kicks at goal, but our defence was too strong

Then we had to go to Warrington for the semi-final and I think they had finished top of the league. That was a really tough match because they were a very strong team.

We beat them 12-7 and what I remember is that they could have won the game if they had chosen to kick the penalties they were given, but Alex Murphy, who was their player-coach, wanted the tries and thought that Warrington didn't need to kick the goals.

Our tackling was fantastic and I bet they regretted not kicking the penalties because they just couldn't get through our defence. It was too strong.

John Clark

Knees up, Harry Beverley

When we went to Warrington for the Championship semi-final everything seemed to click. It seemed that the team expected to win, even though Warrington had a very strong team.

They were very good up front with some very powerful forwards. Where we were standing there were some Warrington supporters complaining about Harry Beverley and his high knee action when he was running. We said he always runs like that, he hasn't just started doing it today. He's done it all his career. Apparently, they thought it wasn't in the spirit of the game.

Geoff Berry

Stones, tears and tickets

I do remember that when we played Warrington in the semi-final and we were returning to Dewsbury on the supporters' coach, we were stoned by the Warrington fans. I was only 14 years old, so it was quite frightening.

The main thing I recall though, was that I was really excited and all I could talk about was getting a ticket for the final. I just kept saying 'We've got to get tickets for the final. I was worried we might not be able to get them because there were a lot of supporters coming out of the woodwork now Dewsbury were doing well and I thought we might miss out.

The end of the semi-final was the first time I had seen my dad cry. Anyway, when we got off the coach back in Dewsbury, Stevo's dad, who had worked with my dad and who had been on the coach, said to me 'Don't worry lad, I'll get you in.'

A few days later, I had just come home from school when I heard someone knocking at the door and when I opened it Stevo was there with two tickets for the final. I said we would pay for them, but he said that there was no need.

Graham Fisher (lifelong Dewsbury fan)

Dewsbury's defence ties up the Wires –
how it was reported in the press

The press reports of Dewsbury's semi-final victory against Warrington largely reinforce the testimony of the Dewsbury players that in this hard-fought match they were able to stifle their opponents, whilst at the same time finding a way to unlock the Warrington defence.

According to The Yorkshire Post, 7th May, 1973, under the heading 'Dewsbury defence holds out': 'It was a typical Dewsbury performance, a triumph for teamwork, tackling and planning.' The report suggests that, fundamentally, Warrington lacked ideas whereas Dewsbury were tightly organised and full of energy, with Adrian Rushton singled out for his stern defence and the Bates brothers, Jeff Grayshon and Mick Stephenson commended for their very high work rate. The article notes that but for the fact that Grayshon had a try disallowed for a forward pass, the victory would have been deservedly more comfortable.

As might be expected, The Dewsbury Reporter, 11th May, 1973, was particularly effusive in its praise of Dewsbury's victory over Warrington. Under the heading 'Fighting Dewsbury tie up the Wires', Doug Booth likened the Dewsbury performance to Sunderland's FA Cup final win against Leeds United that year.

According to Doug: 'Dewsbury outpaced and outshone their number one place opponents.' He also paid tribute to the Dewsbury defence and the overall resilience of the team, noting that the defence 'remained resolute and the forwards tackled like demons as Warrington tightened the screws in the second half,' adding that when Dewsbury had gone behind and may have been about to lose heart, Adrian Rushton 'hit back with the sort of try great players dream about.' Nigel Stephenson had to depart from the field due to an injury, leaving Dick Lowe to assume the kicking duties. When Lowe sealed the victory with a final goal, Doug Booth could not resist the pun that it was a 'fair cop', a reference to Lowe's job as a policeman.

In contrast to The Yorkshire Post and The Dewsbury Reporter, The Liverpool Echo, 7th May, 1973, as might be expected from a Lancashire paper, focused on the fact that for the first time in five years Lancashire had no representation in the Championship final.

It referred to Dewsbury's victory as a 'shock win against Warrington', but noted that they were 'one of the most improved teams in the game over the past few seasons.'

2.

PREPARATION FOR THE FINAL

THERE WAS A *two-week gap between the Championship semi-final and the final because the Challenge Cup final was scheduled for the intervening Saturday, 12th May 1973. Consequently, the team, under the guidance of coach Tommy Smales and his assistant Keith Goulding, had time to prepare for the showdown with Leeds, the team which had decisively defeated them in the Yorkshire Cup final, earlier in the season.*

Fitness training and strategy

There was very little communication between myself and the club committee about preparations so I was able to go ahead and do my own thing. We had beaten Warrington at their ground in the semi-final (12-7) in what was a fantastic game. That meant that we had two weeks to get ready for the final.

During the season we had played 34 league games, 4 Yorkshire Cup games and 3 Championship play-off games, so it was going to be our 42nd match. We'd often played at the weekend and then a midweek game on a Wednesday night, so I just followed the same pattern of preparation as for any game, nothing specific. The players would loosen up and then train to maintain their speed and fitness. I would talk to them about set moves we were developing and then get feedback from Nigel and Mick Stephenson and others. There was very good communication. I learned the importance of that from my job. I ran courses when I worked at the colliery. In training, me and the players learnt as we went along, often from our mistakes, so we saw how to improve moves. In the week before the final, we did some stamina training, sprint training and running through moves.

Of course, all the players were doing full-time jobs, so it was important not to hammer them in training because it would be of no benefit. I just put in one extra session and very much tried to approach it as just another game. The players appreciated this, I think, knowing I wasn't going to flog them.

When we trained, we were not allowed to use the match field at Crown Flatt because the club directors were worried we might cut it up, but I used to sneak the players on to practise moves because it was better to do that on the actual field.

In the build-up, I emphasised the importance of preventing Leeds from getting the ball wide, because Leeds had two international wingers, Atkinson and Smith, who could destroy us if they got some space on the outside of our wingers.

We'd lost heavily to Leeds in the Yorkshire Cup final the previous autumn, so I emphasised that we had to learn from that game. In the end, neither Leeds winger scored, so we got that tactic right.

Tommy Smales

We were a fit team

I don't recall any specific training for the Championship final. We carried on as normal. I think we altered one of the moves so that instead of the ball going to Harry Beverley after a dummy it went to Dick Lowe. We always spent a lot of time practising the moves so that we got them down to a tee.

Our coach, Tommy Smales, was very keen on that. Jeff Grayshon and me were great friends, though at first I wasn't that keen on him because he whacked me in training, but then we stayed mates for 50 years. We worked well together in the pack, both good tacklers.

We were a fit team and Tommy put us through it in training, but we were also playing twice a week in the run up. There was a two-week gap between the semi and the final, so we had a bit more time to prepare.

Joe Whittington

Supplementary training

I worked behind a desk in the office at Yorkshire Copper Works, so didn't do a manual job, but in addition to training on Tuesday and Thursday evening I could do some training in the lunch hour because there were facilities at work. The firm had its own sports club with its own fields.

Training sessions at Dewsbury involved fitness training, moves and an emphasis on teamwork. We didn't do any weight training, but had to run carrying another player on our back.

Allan Agar

Sympathy for those with manual jobs

The training we did was enjoyable. I maintained fitness from it and also the matches of course. I didn't have a manual job, so felt sorry for those who did and then had to come training two nights a week.

In addition to practising the moves, we did fitness exercises and stamina training, but it was nothing exceptional and we didn't alter it for the final.

John Bates

Light training and a walk to Odsal

I am asthmatic, suffer from bronchitis, and wasn't able to train on the Tuesday before the final. Dewsbury told me to rest and take three days off. I came back on Friday, but I didn't really train that week. Tommy told me to stay at home and then I did a bit of light training.

We got together on the Saturday morning and went through all the moves with Tommy. I wasn't fully fit, but Tommy said to give it all I'd got for the first 40 minutes and take it from there.

We didn't want to change anything in the immediate build-up to the final and stopped the coach about 200 yards from Odsal, as we had for the Challenge Cup semi-final, so that we could walk to the ground and get some fresh air.

We liked to do that when we were playing away games. Before a home game I used to walk through Dewsbury market on a Saturday morning to relax. I knew most of the stallholders and they wished me luck before the Championship final.

Mike 'Stevo' Stephenson

Concern about high kicks

I knew that Tommy was a bit worried about whether Greg Ashcroft would drop the ball if Leeds kicked it to him, because he wasn't all that good at catching it. He was fast, though, probably faster than their wingers, internationals. We thought they wouldn't be able to run past him on the outside but knew he'd get some high kicks.

Jeff Grayshon

Frothing at the mouth

We did some fitness training with assistant coach Keith Goulding. He had come from Featherstone with Tommy and had a reputation for being strict. He more or less ran the sessions.

While getting us fit he would join in with us, so led by example.

Tommy worked out the tactics, but it was Keith who ran the training. By the end, he would be frothing at the mouth form the effort, but he made sure that the players did the drills.

There was no slacking.

John Clark

21

Treatment for an injury

I got injured in the semi-final against Warrington, a knee injury, but not a really serious one. Even so, it wasn't a certainty that I would be able to play in the Championship final. I was having treatment all week beforehand.

I hadn't noticed the knock during the game against Warrington, but that wasn't unusual because you often didn't notice them until after the game. As a result, I didn't do much training in the build-up. I was treated by the physio, Jimmy Greenall, who later went off to Penrith with Stevo.

Compared with what they do now, the treatment was pretty basic; just a mixture of electro pads, ice, heat lamp and alternation between heat and cold. On one occasion, earlier in the season, the physio just put some comfrey leaves on my knee and then held them in place with bandaging and left it for 24 hours.

Nigel Stephenson

The planned moves

Absolutely integral to Dewsbury's strategy were the planned moves that were the brainchild of coach Tommy Smales, who devoted considerable time and effort to working out how his team could break down the opposition's defence by catching their players off balance.

Such were the technicalities involved in their execution that Tommy restricted player involvement to those who could best master the intricacies within the context of a free-flowing game.

None of this went unnoticed in the press, as is attested by the 7th May 1973 edition of The Yorkshire Post *and its report on Dewsbury's Championship semi-final win against Warrington.*

According to the article, it was one of Dewsbury's famed moves, when the score was 7-5 to Warrington, which undid the home defence and allowed Nigel Stephenson to score.

Moves developed gradually

This was the third year I'd been with the team and I introduced new moves every season.

I developed moves when playing at Featherstone. I remember on one occasion in training, I said to our scrum half, Carl Dooler, when you are the acting halfback just pass to me and then run round me and that will open up a gap in the defence. Well, in our next match Carl did exactly that and he scored three tries against Dewsbury.

I was the coach of the A team at Dewsbury and when Dave Cox moved to Australia the Dewsbury committee called me in and I thought they were going to sack me because the A team hadn't won a game, but they offered me the job of first team coach.

I introduced some moves straight away, but we lost the first two matches so I went back to basics and gradually introduced different moves. I used to spend a lot of time thinking about new moves, ones which were initially linked to tap penalties but then I started to incorporate them into open play.

Tommy Smales

The moves and teamwork

We were known for our moves. Tommy identified weaknesses in the opposition and the moves were designed to catch our opponents out so as to create opportunities for us.

The moves involved quite a number of players and were based on good teamwork. Tommy was an advanced thinker when it came to setting things up to defeat the opposition. When he was watching matches he could see things that the players couldn't see. The moves involved decoy runners, dummies and drop-offs and run arounds.

Not all the players were involved in the moves, but it was a team effort. The moves didn't rely on just one player but me, Alan Bates and Stevo were involved in quite a few. We weren't the quickest team, so the moves were used to break down the opposition defence and we didn't just use them in the final.

We tried to target the weakest defender. Tommy created a team that gelled together and we were happy to follow his instructions. He reminded us of what was planned, such as to make sure that we got John Bates running wide.

Allan Agar

Drafted out and done to perfection

It was Tommy who instigated the moves. He drafted them out and then showed them to us, though we didn't always understand them at first. We had about six moves and they involved dummy runners, run arounds and switching directions.

Often, I received the ball as a centre, because it worked best that way. Mick Stephenson was the captain and he would call the moves and then we all knew what we had to do.

The idea was to catch the opposition off balance so sometimes the ball was swung in the opposite direction and that created gaps. I was in the second row with Jeff Grayshon, but I had started as a winger, so I had a bit of pace.

In training we got the moves off pat. They were done to perfection because Tommy wouldn't settle for less than that.

John Bates

Fish 'n' chips and abracadabra

Tommy Smales, our coach, was mad on moves and we had so many that I thought I'd better write some on my arm. We had different names for them all, but I can't remember exactly what they were.

It might have been things like 'fish 'n' chips', abracadabra, 'boiled onions', that sort of thing and I would call them out. When we played Featherstone, we hit them with all the moves and they all came off.

There was one outrageous move where I would pretend to throw the ball to the left and then send a pass 20 yard or so to the fullback on the right which would have the defence on the wrong foot.

After training we would sit for hours with Tommy Smales and the assistant coach, who were good mates from when they had been at Featherstone. The assistant coach would have the salt and pepper on the table and he would be moving them around to illustrate the moves. I used to say that if it doesn't work and we're in the wrong position, we'll get hammered; especially in those days when you were likely to get your head knocked off!

Tommy and his assistant were very precise though. Well, we put on three or four of these moves in the first 10 minutes against Featherstone, which was unusual, and it took them by surprise. We got ahead and had the momentum and they were not able to recover.

Mike 'Stevo' Stephenson

I backed up the planned moves

Tommy had us going through the moves that he had taught us and he told us that if we got them right in the final we'd get some chances to score. Mick Stephenson was our best player and he was involved in a lot of the moves.

When we did them, teams were confused because they didn't know what was happening. I used to watch for someone making a break and then I'd try to back them up, because although I was playing in the forwards by then, I was still pretty quick.

When I started at Dewsbury, I played at centre or fullback and I had a bit of pace. Tommy got me to play in the forwards and that helped to make my career.

Jeff Grayshon

Dragging players out of position

We practised some moves, because Tommy had planned particular moves which involved Alan Bates and Mick Stephenson, who were the ball handlers, and a couple of other players. The moves were designed to throw the other team off balance to drag the players out of position and get them moving in the wrong direction.

I used to back Dick Lowe up and he would slip the ball to me. Mick Stephenson used to back me up because he was very fast for a hooker and he could outpace the defence.

John Clark

The Heavy Woollen Victories

Anticipation and speculation

Dewsbury were the undoubted underdogs going into the final, though a quiet confidence had been developing within the team through the course of the play-offs.

Nonetheless, they were to face the mighty Leeds, a star-studded team who'd beaten Dewsbury 36-9 in the previous autumn's Yorkshire Cup final. Unsurprisingly, there was a degree of apprehension amongst some members of the Dewsbury team, which is not to say that they felt that victory was impossible. Equally, there were those who believed that, having progressed to the final, Dewsbury could now seize their chance.

We didn't realise how good we were

Of course, Leeds were a much bigger club, the richest team, so the newspapers thought that we didn't have much chance. They were a team of internationals, but most of our players, apart from Mick Stephenson, were not well known.

There is no question about it that they had better individual players, but collectively, as a team, we were better. I think that Leeds had already peaked that season, but we had been getting better with each game in the play-offs and that was an important difference. The newspapers and Leeds underestimated us.

Derek Turner was the Leeds coach and the final was his last game at Leeds. They were probably pleased that they had got us instead of Warrington. They had beaten St Helens in the semi-final, but they might have thought that our match had taken more out of us.

In a way, we didn't realise how good we were and how well we were playing. In the last matches before the play-offs we played Rochdale away and our forwards were ploughing down the middle and we hammered them and they were not an easy team to play on their ground. We played Hull away, midweek, and you know how difficult it was to play at the Boulevard in front of that crowd in the Threepenny Stand. Nobody was keen to play there.

I think that the newspapers had missed how much progress the team was making towards the end of the season and in the first couple of rounds of the play-offs.

Tommy Smales

Man for man they were better than us

We were definitely the underdogs going into the game. At least the *Dewsbury Reporter* had a headline which said 'Go in there lads tomorrow and win.' I remember listening to Radio Leeds and hearing Derek Turner, the Leeds coach, say something like 'I don't know why Dewsbury are bothering to turn up.'

Well, that just motivated us even more. We knew that man for man they were better than us. They were a team of international players, either players who had already played at international level or did so in the future. There was John Holmes, Alan Smith, Syd Hynes, Les Dyl, John Atkinson, Alan Hardisty, Keith Hepworth, Tony Fisher, Phil Cookson... Ray Batten wasn't playing, but if you look at numbers 1 to 7, that was some team.

They must have had 12 internationals or future internationals in that team, whereas there was only Stevo in our team who, at that time, had played at international level. Eventually, there were five others who went on to be internationals: me, Alan Bates, John Bates, Jeff Grayshon and Harry Beverley. We weren't expected to win, but that didn't matter to us because we knew we were well prepared.

Nigel Stephenson

They've got no chance

When we got down onto the pitch and lined up, I looked at Jeff and said we're going to win today. They think they're going to beat us but they've got no chance. We were a great defensive side, even though, at the time, Mick Stephenson, never thought that we were a great side. I did. Mick used to sweep up behind the main tacklers.

I used to joke that I did all his tackling for him and that's why he's so good at talking!

Joe Whittington

We'd done very well to reach the final

Nobody expected us to beat Leeds because they had a top class team. The general feeling was that we had done very well to reach the final but Leeds would be too fast and powerful.

We knew that Tommy had watched Leeds and that he would have been on the lookout for weaknesses. We had a really good team spirit and that was down to Tommy.

John Bates

I didn't know whether it would be enough

The newspapers didn't give us a chance against Leeds. I can see why Leeds were favourites because they had umpteen players who were well-known and quite a lot who were internationals.

Mick Stephenson was our only well-known player, but we had beaten two top teams to get to the final, so I thought it wasn't right that the papers weren't giving us any chance of winning. I didn't expect us to win because I looked at the Leeds team with players like Syd Hynes, John Atkinson, Terry Clawson and Tony Fisher.

I wanted to win and I knew that I was going to get stuck in and try to knock them off their game, but I didn't know whether it would be enough.

Jeff Grayshon

I hoped we wouldn't get hammered

I used to have a lot of newspaper clippings from the *Dewsbury Reporter* about the build-up to the match and the final itself, but I don't know what's happened to them.

I do remember that in the reporting in the newspapers it was all pretty low key with regard to Dewsbury – little Dewsbury against the mighty Leeds. Of course, Leeds were in their pomp and they had a fantastic team, full of international players. I mean Dewsbury had a really good team, but the players were not as well-known as the Leeds players.

Mick Stephenson was already an international and then there were others who went on to play at international level. I was really excited about going to the final but I was not expecting Dewsbury to win. I hoped that we wouldn't get hammered, but Leeds were one of the top teams.

Graham Fisher (lifelong Dewsbury fan)

Predictably, The Dewsbury Reporter, 11th May 1973, was quite bullish about Dewsbury's chances against Leeds.

Under the heading "Same again – but watch us this time Leeds", R Stansfield warned Leeds to expect something rather different to their experience in the Yorkshire Cup final against Dewsbury last autumn, and cautioned them not to be complacent. He pointed out that Dewsbury had markedly improved since they had suffered a heavy defeat at the hands of Leeds in that Yorkshire Cup final and that they had, without the fanfare associated with more fashionable clubs, been quietly growing in confidence.

Michael Lumb was quoted as saying that Dewsbury "are far better equipped than in October 1972", adding that Dewsbury "have come of age."

In The Yorkshire Post, 18th May 1973, under the heading "Dewsbury aim to make it third time lucky", Alfred Drewry is rather more circumspect about Dewsbury's prospects in the Championship final. The reference in the title was to Dewsbury's loss in both the Yorkshire Cup final and the Challenge Cup semi-final. It was pointed out that Dewsbury would be the first club to win the Championship final having finished as low as 8th. They would surpass Halifax, who had won from 7th place in 1965.

In the article, Mike Lumb, the Dewsbury president, drew attention to the fact that Dewsbury had already beaten the teams that finished 1st and 2nd in the league, Warrington and Featherstone respectively, so he saw no reason why Dewsbury couldn't beat Leeds, who had finished 3rd. Lumb highlighted a lack of experience as the main reason why Dewsbury had not prevailed in those two previous crucial games, the Yorkshire Cup final and the semi-final of the Challenge Cup.

Nonetheless, the article contrasted Leeds' familiarity with success with the fact that Dewsbury had not won anything since the 1946-1947 season. The importance of Nigel Stephenson's scoring ability was foregrounded as a key element of Dewsbury's recent success.

Addtionally, Jack Myerscough, the Leeds chairman, dismissed any suggestion of complacency with the comment: "So far as we are concerned, the record Yorkshire Cup final victory over Dewsbury might as well have taken place ten years ago."

Interestingly, The Liverpool Echo, 18th May, 1973, which had no skin in the game, as it were, under the heading "Dewsbury seek revenge victory", suggested, somewhat presciently, that the abilities of Mick and Nigel Stephenson might propel Dewsbury to victory, noting that if Dewsbury settled down quickly and retained possession, they could spring a surprise.

3.

THE CHAMPIONSHIP FINAL – 19th MAY 1973

FOR MANY PLAYERS who have played in the final of a significant competition an overriding memory is that the game went by very quickly, but at the same time there are key moments for each player that will forever stay in their memory. For the coach, an important final is likely to be a more gruelling affair mentally than it is for the players, in so far as the coach's ability to influence the game once it is in progress is limited. Nonetheless, for players and coach alike, recollections of a significant victory are very satisfying indeed.

He just ran away from the defence

The highlights of the game for me were the Dewsbury tries because they came from moves that we had rehearsed. Allan Agar's came from a move near the line which caused a gap to open up, but in fact we'd only completed half of the set move but a gap opened up, so Allan went through it.

Nigel's try was similar, but my favourite was Mick Stephenson's second try because he just ran away from the defence and they couldn't deal with him. His first try came from a lovely passing move and that got us going.

They came back at us, which is what I expected and we were helped by Hardisty being sent off in the first half. It was a stiff-arm tackle and after the referee had talked to the touch judge he made a quick decision. I think that it was the only time in his career that Hardisty was sent off.

When Leeds got their third try, I thought they might have a chance of winning. I was just hoping that my players wouldn't lose their concentration. I was thinking we need to be on top of our game all the time for the full 80 minutes because they are a team of internationals and all it needs is one little slip.

It was nerve wracking for me on the sidelines because towards the end we were tiring a bit as a result of using so much energy and general wear and tear in the match. Dick Lowe had to come off with an injury, so I put on Brian Taylor, but after the game some members of the Dewsbury committee said why didn't you put Steve Lee on so he could have some time playing in the final. I didn't think that Steve would be able to complete as many tackles as we needed and if he had made a mistake with a tackle that could have led to a try.

The Committee members said that I could have put him on for the last few minutes, just for sentimental reasons so he could say he had played in the final, but I didn't want to take any risks.

It just shows that you are not going to be able to please everybody, even when you win.

Tommy Smales

It sucked the life out of Leeds

Leeds went into the lead with a penalty, but they didn't score a try in the first half. We scored in the first 15 minutes. It was a quick passing move which ended with me passing inside to Stevo, who raced away to score near the posts.

Then, before half-time, Allan Agar scored a try from one of our set moves which was started off by Stevo. We hadn't gone right through the move, but when Allan Agar got the ball a gap had opened up and he ran straight through it to score. Allan was a good player and a great bloke. He came from Featherstone and he looked after me at Dewsbury because I was just a young lad and he made sure that I was protected.

We were leading 12-4 at half-time because I had converted the tries and dropped a goal as well. In the second half Stevo scored an unbelievable try where he just ran away from the defence.

Leeds scored a try and then the one in the last quarter I scored under the posts from one of our moves, started off by Stevo, meant that was that. The crowd and the players were going wild. All our tries had been scored near the posts, so I had been able to kick all the conversions, plus a drop-goal.

We did get a bit worried when Leeds got those quick tries and were on a bit of a roll, but that try I scored came from one of our run-arounds and that sucked the life out of Leeds.

Of course, we were helped by Hardisty getting sent off, but it was a sending off offence and he didn't argue with it. It wasn't malicious, but it was a stiff-arm tackle and it could have taken one of our team out of the game. We were leading at the time when he was sent off.

There were some great performances. We had a fantastic team spirit. Everybody knew the job they had to do and did it. We had a great defence. I played in the centre but I was all over the field trying to create breaks and making tackles. Harry Beverley had a great game. He ran hard with his back straight and his knees lifted up high. He was one of our unsung heroes.

It was a great win for Trevor 'Dick' Lowe, our oldest player. He had been in the old Dewsbury team and really deserved his medal. Solid as a rock, he was good at passing the ball, a good pair of hands.

Nigel Stephenson

I flattened Geoff Clarkson

Our main strategy was to keep them out, stop them getting the ball to the wings and take any chances we created. We scored a try in the first 15 minutes. It was Mick Stephenson, taking a pass from Nigel.

It gave them a shock. Mick wasn't the best hooker in the business, but got his share of the ball apart from when we played Huddersfield and he was up against Don Close. Mick used to say that we wouldn't be getting much ball that day. Don Close used to kick him and stamp on his foot. Mick was fast though, especially over the first 30 yards. He was an international and deserved to be. He had a great game in the final and deserved the man of the match. When we scored our second try the ball should have come to me from a Mick Stephenson run around, but a gap had opened up and the ball went to Allan Agar and he went through it and scored.

One moment I particularly remember was when I flattened Geoff Clarkson with a tackle. It was a fair tackle, but he came short from the left hand side and I met him head on and he went flat on his back. I wasn't that big for a second row/loose forward, only about 13st 12lbs, but I've got a long body and short legs, which is ideal for tackling.

When I went to a St John Fishers reunion, a bloke who was at school with me and was a Dewsbury supporter said that he loved my tackling. I could tackle anything. That's why my nose has been broken a few times. During the game, I made sure I kept away from Syd Hynes, unless it couldn't be avoided, because I'd had one or two do's before with Syd and I didn't want to risk getting sent off.

At half-time we stayed on the field because it was too far to walk back up to the changing rooms and you might sprain your ankle coming back down all those steps. David Ward, who I know, came on in the second half because Fisher was injured. He was four years younger than me, but he used to train with us at Shaw Cross because he was that good. Derek Turner had dropped David Jeanes and chose Eccles or Clarkson in his place. I think Jeanes would have been more dangerous.

Joe Whittington

Struck by the size of the crowd

Greg said that he was very worried about dropping the ball in the final, because in a few reports about who would win the final there had been suggestions that Greg was likely to drop the ball when he was catching it from a kick. He was very pleased that this didn't happen. He was very keen on figures (statistics) connected to the games he played in and he had loads of scrapbooks.

He was struck by how big the crowd was at Odsal, especially since nobody had expected Dewsbury to get there. He said it was much bigger than any crowd he'd played in front of before. He was proud of his medal because this was the biggest game of his career.

Diane Ashcroft (Greg Ashcroft's widow)

The game went by so quickly

One of the things I remember most about this game was that Alan Hardisty got sent off and this was probably the only time in his career that he got sent off. He wasn't that sort of player.

The game went by so quickly probably because our concentration level was so high. The moves that we had practised worked. We didn't always score from them but they helped to open up gaps and that's how we got some of our tries.

Leeds probably thought that it was going to be easy, but the moves we had practised were all spot on this time, which wasn't always the case. We surprised them and they couldn't recover.

Stevo was our best player. He wasn't the best hooker as far as winning the ball from the scrum goes, but he was great in the loose.

He wore a corset in some of the games because of his back and that's probably why he wasn't as good as some hookers as a ball getter.

Allan Agar

You jumped in the air

Dewsbury started with moves as soon as they got into the Leeds half. I remember looking at the video of the game and when you scored you jumped in the air and celebrated in front of the crowd.

I don't remember you ever doing that again.

Richard Agar (Allan's son), to his father

Hardisty didn't argue

Tommy thought that we would be able to catch them off guard with our moves.

On one of the moves I received the ball, running wide in the centre and I was stiff armed by Alan Hardisty. The ref sent him straight off. He didn't have much choice really and Hardisty didn't argue. I think that it was the only time he was sent off in his career. When I was picked to play on the tour to Australia and New Zealand I came across Alan because he was coaching at Rockhampton. He remembered that I was the one who got him sent off.

We used the same six moves in the final with Mick calling them out and they worked very well. Leeds were caught off balance and once we got away from them they couldn't recover. I remember that the game was fast and furious and although I didn't expect us to win, I knew that we would do our very best. We certainly felt on top of the world after beating Warrington, so we weren't afraid of Leeds.

John Bates

I had a right ding-dong in the scrum

Of course, we were the underdogs and the press didn't really give us a chance, especially as Leeds had hammered us in the Yorkshire Cup final. Anyway, we put all the moves on right from the start and we got them on the back foot. They were taken by surprise.

When I saw that the Leeds players were starting to argue amongst themselves, I knew that we were going to win. Hardisty was sent off for the high tackle on John Bates and that did help us, but I thought that we had the game won by then.

I scored the first try from an inside pass from Nigel and that gave us some momentum. That was after about ten minutes and it was the first try of the game. Nigel had a good sidestep. He didn't wait until he got right up to the man, but sidestepped as he saw the tackler moving across and changed the direction of the attack. I followed him when he went through and he just slipped me a short pass for me to go under the posts.

They'd kicked a penalty. Tommy had told us that we had to shock them and put them on the back foot. I don't remember the names we used for the moves but they worked. I mean they were a team of internationals and they were probably not expecting what they got from us.

At that time, I was the only international in our team. After the loss to Bradford in the Challenge Cup, we were determined not to let that happen again. Some of the older players had been in tears after that game. It was a question of guts and determination and the moves we had practised. We had to make sure, as well, that Leeds didn't get going, so we had to tackle very well. After that first try, I kept telling the team that we had got Leeds.

I had a right ding-dong in the scrum with Tony Fisher. If there was ever a lunatic who played rugby, it was Tony Fisher. I remember calling out the moves and that we didn't drop the ball. They went smoothly. When I scored my second try in the second half I noticed that the Leeds players hadn't got into position properly so I called for our tackled player to play the ball quickly. From acting half-back I passed the ball to Alan Bates and then he passed back to me and the Leeds defence just seemed to open up. I had a bit of pace so they couldn't get to me before I scored. The try that Allan Agar scored just before half time came from one of our set moves. The Leeds defence just seemed to open up and Allan went through a wide gap. They just weren't expecting what we were able to throw at them.

I operated as a sweeper behind the main line of tacklers. This was Tommy's idea so that I could cut down anyone who broke through, or field any short kicks that were put in the gap between our main line of defence and our fullback. I didn't mind that because it meant that I did less tackling than the other forwards and less than I had to do when playing for the county or for GB. Adrian Rushton covered behind me, anticipating where they might put longer kicks. It's probably the case that if our moves hadn't come off we would have lost. But they did and I called out where I wanted the players to be and they all did their jobs to perfection.

We had tags with our numbers on held round our socks and as we climbed the steps back up to the dressing rooms at Odsal at the end of the game our fans were grabbing them and tearing them off as souvenirs. Someone gave me their scarf and I was still wearing it when I lifted the trophy.

Mike 'Stevo' Stephenson

The Leeds players were all over the place at half-time

I remember when we went down from the changing rooms to the pitch being a bit worried about coming a cropper down the steps because they were very steep and lots of them.

I played for Bradford later on and I was always very careful about walking down the steps. That's probably why I didn't really notice any Dewsbury fans in the crowd because I was concentrating too much on going down the steps.

Once we got ahead and Leeds weren't getting on top of us, I was starting to think that we could do it. One of the main things I was trying to do was not to miss any tackles because we knew that if Leeds broke through our defence, they could get the ball to players like Hardisty who we wouldn't be able to catch. He was great at backing up and once he got the ball in the open, he was gone. When he got sent off for a stiff arm on John Bates, I was thinking that we can definitely do them now. When Allan Agar scored before half-time, I could see Leeds players' heads go down. They seemed to be a bit bamboozled about what was happening to them.

I do remember that Tommy Smales got us all together on the field at half-time because it was too far back up to the changing rooms. He gathered us round him and he said we just had to stick to what we had been doing. He said that Leeds were rattled but that they would come back at us, so we had to keep tackling like we had been doing. He said that we had to stop them throwing the ball about, to get on top of them and frustrate them.

He said that Leeds didn't seem to be able to work out what was happening. We'd knocked them off balance and they didn't know what to do about it. He told us to just keep at it and make sure that they couldn't get the ball out to the wingers. We were all together at half-time, but out of the corner of my eye I could see that the Leeds players were all over the place and when I thought about it later, that was a big difference between us and Leeds in that match. We had a great team spirit and that helped to win us the game that day.

Leeds did come back at us and they scored some tries, but I can't remember who scored them. I can remember that they didn't kick many goals and we had got a drop goal. I had a few runs and so did Harry Beverley, who ran with his knees up and was hard to tackle.

Me and my mate Joe Whittington got stuck into tackling as much as we could. Everybody did their bit and that's why we won. All the things we had practised during training sessions came off that day. I suppose that we might have looked like mugs if they hadn't. We did some knock-ons because you always do, but we didn't make any mistakes with the moves.

I don't remember all that much about the end of the match apart from that we were jumping about on the pitch. It's all a bit of a blur.

There are some photos of us holding the cup and I can remember that as we went back up to the dressing rooms there were Dewsbury fans who were near the steps and they were patting us on the back as we walked up the steps. If you'd lost a game at Odsal it felt like you were going up a mountain when you were going back up all those steps, but I didn't really notice it after we had won that cup.

Jeff Grayshon

I watched it for the first time after more than 40 years

I watched the final for the first time fairly recently. I hadn't seen it before. My son downloaded it from his phone onto the TV and I was very impressed by our performance.

I mean, I knew it must have been good when I played in the match, because we beat a very strong side, but looking at it for the first time, after more than 40 years, I was so impressed with our tackling and particularly the tackling done by the forwards. We didn't give them many opportunities and they couldn't break through or throw the ball about.

When you're on the field you don't see the moves in the same way, but when I watched it on TV I could see that the moves we put on worked because the Leeds players were dragged out of position and they couldn't recover.

I could see that Mick Stephenson deserved the 'Man of the Match' award. They couldn't contain him at all and he was too fast for their forwards. Alan Hardisty was sent off, but I don't think that was the reason why we won. We were ahead before he was sent off and we were getting the better of Leeds. I mean they had enough top players to be able to cope.

Their forwards didn't match ours. They couldn't wear us down. Their star players didn't really get into the game. You hardly saw Syd Hynes and their wingers didn't get any chances. When Hardisty was sent off, they must have been thrown off balance a bit, but we outplayed them. We had an excellent team spirit and we worked for each other and that was why we won.

I've still got my medal. It's the only one I've got, but when I think about it, we might have won three cups that season. We lost to Leeds in the final of the Yorkshire Cup and then we lost to Bradford in the semi-final of the Challenge Cup and then they lost to Featherstone and we had beaten Featherstone in the Championship quarter final.

John Clark

John Clark's perspective is an interesting one, coming from someone who played in the Championship final, but whose reflections are based on his viewing of the game for the first time, more than 40 years after he had played in it.

For the players, as indicated earlier, the game went by in a flash, but this is not usually the experience of fans observing from the terraces, particularly with regard to the tense final minutes of a game.

We didn't buy our tickets in advance

Five of us used to travel to the away games by car and we'd get there for 1:00pm for a 3:00pm start so we could absorb the atmosphere and get talking to people. We used to stay for an hour after the match in order to let the traffic go down, so we made a day of it.

We didn't buy our tickets in advance, we just paid on the gate.

Odsal was never going to be full. I think that the following year we bought tickets in advance for Bradford and Warrington, but if the five of us paid on the gate we knew that we would be able to stand together. We stood on the terrace next to the steps the players came down. We were about halfway up the terrace. Later on, I walked up and down those steps as a referee. It was a daunting journey.

Geoff Berry (lifelong Dewsbury fan and former referee)

Alan Bates looked like he was buzzing

We got to the ground good and early to make sure that we got a good spot, though we didn't deliberately choose to be near the steps so that we could congratulate the players at the end.

The crowd built gradually and we were getting some stick from the Leeds fans; there was no trouble, it was just banter. When the players came down the steps we noticed straightaway that they had garters on their socks with an advertising tag attached. We'd never seen that before and two weeks later John Bates told me that the garters were from a firm in Heckmondwike who had given the garters to Mick Stephenson. He was only a little guy, but we used to say that when Alan Bates doesn't play Dewsbury don't play. We often struggled without him. Steve Lee stood in for him and he didn't do badly, but we always missed Alan. Alan made things tick, because a lot of the moves came through him. He was a really nice guy. He was one of the lads and always had time for everyone. He didn't think he was above anyone else.

The whole team looked relaxed that day, even though Leeds were strong favourites. Leeds were a big unit and they had plenty of international players, but we contained them very well. As the game went on you could feel that the Dewsbury supporters were getting more confident. The team was competing well and the players' confidence increased and that transferred to the supporters. Obviously, when Harry Hunt sent off Alan Hardisty, that was an important turning point which boosted the fans' confidence and this rubbed off on the players. There was a buzz around the ground amongst Dewsbury supporters.

The players recognised that they had an opportunity. The didn't just start throwing the ball around willy nilly. They stuck to the plan and wore Leeds down, especially as Leeds were a man short, which takes a lot out of the team.

It was a fantastic team effort and that was down to the marvellous team spirit. That's how the spectators saw it. Stevo got the 'man of the match' because of the tries he scored, but they were all heroes. Dick Lowe's tackling was outstanding. A lot didn't realise how important he was as the second man in the tackle, smothering the ball and stopping it being recycled. Dewsbury had a particular pattern with Stevo in a sweeper position between the main defence line and the fullback. This meant that Stevo could conserve energy because he didn't need to do as much tackling as the other forwards, so when he got the ball he could run 40 yards at full pace when opposition forwards were tiring. I don't know who came up with that, but I imagine it was Tommy Smales.

Geoff Berry (lifelong Dewsbury fan and former referee)

It helps to revive my spirits

We went to Odsal on a supporters' bus that we got on at Long Causeway, the other side of the road from the bus station.

The bus was full and there were quite a few coaches there for the fans. We got to the ground in good time because my dad always liked to have a pint before the game. (These days you need more than a couple of pints to watch Dewsbury.) There was a pub near the ground, just outside Odsal stadium and my dad went in there with some other blokes. Me and some other kids waited outside, as you did, with a bottle of pop and a packet of crisps, as you did whilst your dad had a pint.

Anyway, we got into the stadium about an hour before the start of the game and there were a lot of Leeds supporters and neutral fans already in there. We were behind the posts at the Rooley Lane end of the ground. There was me, my dad, my uncle and a couple of my dad's workmates. It was packed and because I'm not very tall and was only 14, I spent quite a lot of time on one of my dad's mates' shoulders. In the end we were a group of Dewsbury supporters surrounded by Leeds fans and some neutrals. The atmosphere will live with me forever. I had been to Wembley but I had never been to Odsal stadium as a fan.

I was struck by the number of Leeds fans who were there, but it wasn't really surprising because Leeds is a big city and they had a lot more supporters than Dewsbury, who didn't have a massive following. They took it well though at the final whistle. I will hand it to them because they stood up and applauded Dewsbury. They were saying "We just didn't turn up today" and they were praising Dewsbury for their performance.

I thought that the rugby we played that day was fantastic; the run around moves with Stevo. I still watch it because it helps to revive my spirits after Dewsbury have had a bad season.

That day, Dewsbury were always in control of the game and I must admit that it surprised me because, as I said before, I was not expecting us to win. I was hoping for a miracle. Dewsbury didn't give anything away and it was all the team. On the day, Leeds just couldn't cope. Perhaps they had expected a fairly easy game and were taken by surprise because they didn't realise that we had some very good players.

Nigel Stephenson was a very underrated player. He had a great footballing brain and a lovely sidestep. I used to think that if players just followed him they would get the ball from him and be able to go through a gap. He could always see which pass to make. He did play at international level and if he had been just a little bit quicker, he would have been world class.

On paper Leeds looked far superior to Dewsbury, man for man. We had some very good players but they had a team of internationals who were used to winning things. Dewsbury had a fantastic team spirit. They all stuck together and if one of them made a mistake, there was no blaming each other. There was no back chat to the referee. They respected the ref and just got on with the game. Back then, you could not mess about with the referee. If there was constant back chat, you would be off the field. (That's the trouble with Paul Sykes. He's constantly in the referee's ear and it costs us).

As much as anything that day, I was impressed by the quality of the rugby that we played, the backing up, the accurate passing and the timing of the moves like the run arounds. I think that Leeds were not expecting that. They were knocked off balance and by the time they steadied themselves it was too late.

Having said that, I wasn't certain that we were going to win until five minutes before the end. You know what it's like, even when you are well in front you are still a bit nervous, you're worried that the opponents might suddenly make a comeback.

I mean Leeds did fight back and I was still a bit nervous ten minutes from the end of the match, thinking that anything could happen because Leeds were a great side. The thing was that everything Dewsbury did that day came off. Leeds were flummoxed and they looked tired. When the final whistle went, I cried and that day I went onto the field and I got a bollocking from my dad because he had told me not to, but me and some other lads just couldn't resist it. There were police there, but they didn't try to stop us getting on to the field and running towards the players.

The neutral spectators were clapping and the Leeds fans said they had been outplayed. One of my dad's workmates who was a lifelong Leeds fan said that it was the first time he'd seen Leeds outplayed and outthought like they had been that day.

Graham Fisher (lifelong fan)

A mixed bag – the press coverage of Dewsbury's historic victory

Rugby league is and always has been a regional sport associated with a northern working-class following, so it is perhaps no surprise that there was very limited coverage of Dewsbury's historic victory in the national newspapers.

The Sunday People, 20th May, 1973, under the heading 'Leeds Jinx Again', included two brief columns, the substance of which was that in both association football and rugby league, teams from Leeds had come up short against inferior opponents. More surprisingly, perhaps, for a newspaper which would have been bought by many northern working-class readers, The Sunday Mirror, 20th May, 1973, under the heading 'HARDISTY IS SENT OFF', recorded only that fact and the score in the Championship final. Indeed, though it had a bigger headline, the article contained fewer words than 'Viva Vivien', a story about the progress of Vivien Saunders in the Tarax professional golf tournament for women in Melbourne. It may be that this was the London edition of the Sunday Mirror!

Alfred Drewry, writing in The Yorkshire Post, 21st May, 1973, under the heading 'Dewsbury take title and show Leeds' flaws', emphasised the workmanlike nature of Dewsbury's triumph, endorsing Mick Stephenson's assessment that, even before Hardisty's dismissal, Dewsbury had demonstrated that they were the superior team. Drewry's assessment was that, whilst they were no world beaters, Dewsbury were supremely efficient, demonstrating careful attention to detail throughout the match.

A rather more complimentary assessment of Dewsbury's performance by Geoff Cockin appeared in The Huddersfield Examiner, 21st May, 1973. Under the heading 'Dewsbury make their mark in rugby league history', Cockin wrote:

'The Dewsbury pack confirmed my forecast of getting the better of the Leeds six in the Rugby League Championship final at Odsal on Saturday, but then confounded the rest of the forecast by overwhelming the Headingley backs as well to win the Championship for the first time in their 75-year history ... such was their dominance that I don't think the sending off of Hardisty could be said to have made the difference between success and failure.

'Dewsbury played with a zest, purpose and dash that Leeds were never able to emulate and the strange thing was that despite their success by 22-13, they might easily have had another two or three tries. They had their chances.'

In The Batley News, 24th May,1973, The only reference to Dewsbury's historic victory occurs in an advert for GB Discounts, Birstall: Well Done Dewsbury Rugby League Club

There was no coverage in the previous edition of the Batley News about the build-up to the Championship Final, whereas when Batley won the Northern Rail Cup in 2010, there was extensive coverage in all the local Heavy Woollen District and Spen Valley newspapers.

By this time all these local newspapers were part of the same group, but it does seem rather churlish that there was no story about Dewsbury's victory, an important triumph for the Heavy Woollen District, in the Batley News.

However, with regard to press coverage of Dewsbury's outstanding victory, it is appropriate to leave the last word to Doug Booth in The Dewsbury Reporter, *25th May 1973. Under the heading 'We are the Champions', Doug wrote:*

'Dewsbury displayed fast attractive football, the like of which left the crowd of 19,000 gasping in amazement and awe. They had the confidence to throw the ball around like basketball players and constantly worried Leeds with their power-packed teamwork.

'It was a fantastic team performance and really it would be wrong of me to single out anyone for special consideration...'

This stands in contrast with Drewry's comments in the Yorkshire Post *and serves to illustrate either the inherent bias of the local Dewsbury newspaper or an attempt at ironic hyperbole by the individual journalist.*

4.

THE WINNING FORMULA

Reasons why Dewsbury defied the odds

THERE ARE A number of interrelated reasons, some of which have already been hinted at in the preceding testimony, which help to explain why, having finished eighth in the table, Dewsbury were able to go on and win the Championship title. In the end, it is the players' performances on the field, both individually and collectively as a team, which determine the results. It is their running, passing, tackling and kicking which enable them to overcome their opponents. The players also implement the team strategy, but a strategy has to be developed in the first place and that is the responsibility of the team coach.

Tommy Smales was a cerebral, innovative and imaginative coach whose planned moves, management of the players and identification of the opposition's weaknesses enabled Dewsbury to outfox teams which, player for player, appeared to be stronger than Dewsbury. Let us therefore begin this section with testimony which reinforces the importance of Tommy Smales' role in Dewsbury's march to victory.

I had a very good rapport with the Dewsbury players

The players responded well to my ideas and I used to get a lot of good feedback. One of the players, who was the captain of the team, was struggling a bit with organising the moves and he said that he was unhappy with the responsibility, so I made Mick Stephenson the captain because he was very capable and ready to take the lead.

Another player, who was as hard as iron, came to me and told me that he found the moves difficult to remember because they were complicated. I said that I would work with him but he still wasn't very happy, so I just used him in one move that was nice and straightforward. It was one in which he took a tap penalty, passed to one of our players and then ran round that player to receive a pass from him before passing to a man running onto the ball. I had a very good rapport with the Dewsbury players and they often made suggestions about how we could improve set plays. I think that because I had only recently retired and I had played against some of the players I was coaching, they respected me because they had seen me in action.

Over the years, I'd thought about the game a lot and I'd picked up things as a player. I'd watched for moves that were good and worked and I talked to players. When I was at Dewsbury I got to know the players' likes and dislikes and tried to ensure that what they liked fit in with my ideas. I think that's why we had a brilliant team spirit, like it was when I played for Featherstone and we won the Challenge Cup in 1967. We beat the top four sides to get to that Final, which shows you what you can do with great team spirit.

Tommy Smales

I could only see it clearly from behind the sticks

I used to spend a lot of time thinking about tactics and specific moves and how to gain an advantage in a match. I liked to watch from different places in the ground in order to get different views of the players movements. I went behind the sticks to look at different widths, especially what the opposition was doing, as the ball was moved across the field. I noticed that when a team was defending against Dewsbury down in the nine hole, if we repeatedly moved the ball back and forth amongst the backs, the opponents' centres came up in a straight line but after a tackle they retreated at an angle and that slippage meant that a gap opened up that we could exploit.

It's much better to run into a gap rather than run at a player. I was only able to see this clearly when I was looking from behind the sticks. I wouldn't have been able to see it from the bench on the touchline.

On one occasion I went up into the stand so that I could get a view of the game from above which enabled me to see the position and movements of both teams. I asked the committee at Dewsbury if I could have two walkie talkies so that I could be up in the stand and communicate with an assistant coach on the bench, because I would be able to see things that he couldn't see but the committee said no because they didn't want to spend money on walkie talkies.

I got the idea from working down the pit where men would use walkie talkies to communicate with each other about the movement of coal in the long tunnels. The committee said that it would cost too much. Of course, the Aussies did that sort of thing long before.

I also suggested that the club should buy heavier boots for the players to use in training in order to improve their speed. My idea was that when they wore lighter boots for a match, they would be able to run faster. It's like they do with racehorses; the horses wear heavier shoes for training than they wear for an actual race. Again, the Dewsbury committee knocked it back because of the expense.

Tommy Smales

A prop rather than a second row forward

Harry Beverley was a great fellah. One night when I went along to organise a training session, Harry was there but there had been no communication from the committee, so I wasn't expecting a new player. A committee member told me that Harry was a second row forward, so I put him there but when I saw him in action on the field, I could see that the second row wasn't his position. I asked him what position he had played at Leeds and he told me that he had been a prop, so I moved him to the front row.

He was as strong as an ox. He worked in a foundry and had really powerful arms from lifting a lot of heavy stuff at work. After one training session when all the players were in the bath, Harry asked for a scrubbing brush and when someone got one for him, he started scrubbing his face with it!

Tommy Smales

I got everything done down on the pitch

I think one of the main reasons why we won the match was that our attitude was better than theirs. Our team spirit was very high and had been lifted up above Leeds' level.

I instructed the team to get on top of their opponents and stop them playing expansive rugby and we did that very effectively in the first half. When we had played at Hull earlier in the season, at half time I didn't take the players off the pitch. I got them in a semi-circle in front of the threepenny stand with their backs to the crowd. Everything went quiet because the Hull fans had not seen anything like that before. I did the same in the final at Odsal because it was too far to walk back up the steps to the changing rooms. I got everything done down on the pitch, plasters, liniment and anything that needed doing and then I gathered the players in a semi-circle in front of the main stand and I told them they'd done very well but it wasn't finished yet. I told them to keep tackling, keep the defence tight and to keep talking to each other to maintain the organisation of the team. I said that they should remember that we had trained hard all season and that we were fitter than Leeds. I told them that Leeds had probably realised that they had been too slack, that they had been thinking it would be easy, but I told the Dewsbury lads that if we stuck to our plan, it would be hard for Leeds to pull back up from scratch.

At half time, Leeds players were wandering about as individuals. Derek hadn't got control of his team like I had with mine.

Tommy Smales

Always the forward thinker

When I was coach at Batley at the end of the 1970s, I said that what we need is to nurture two or three Pakistani players to expand our local support, but nobody was interested.

I wanted to have a system which involved specialist man to man, individual training at Batley, but to do that I needed some assistants. All the clubs were interested in was how much it would cost. I said that it could be £5 per week for each one plus a free pass to home matches, suggesting that this would be beneficial to the club because the assistants might bring along their families or mates to the matches. Mick Lumb, who had been chairman at Dewsbury when I was there and was now at Batley, wasn't interested.
Tommy Smales

He was ahead of his time

Tommy Smales, the coach, and his assistant were unbelievable for getting us fit. Tommy's sidekick used to run us to death, so we knew that Leeds wouldn't be any fitter than us.

I know it's been said before about coaches in other sports, but it's still true that Tommy Smales was 'a coach before his time.' He was a thinker who worked out moves and urged his players to follow the ball so that they would be in a position to take a pass. He wasn't a shouter, he talked to players and listened to any ideas they had so that they were involved in developing the moves he introduced. We had runarounds, switches in direction. We all had individual jobs to do and we carried them out as well as working together as a team.
Nigel Stephenson

He helped us to relax

We were playing as good football as ever before the Championship final and Tommy got us in the right frame of mind for the game. We knew that man for man we were not as good as some of the other teams, so we had a very relaxed manner and it worked. Hardly anybody thought that we had a chance of winning and Tommy took all the pressure off us. He made us laugh and that helped us to relax.

Allan Agar

He was calm and measured

Tommy was a very good coach. He thought a lot about the game and he wasn't like some coaches who were shouting and bawling. He was very calm and measured. Maurice Bamforth used to crack players across the head at halftime, but not those who knew he would crack him back. He didn't do it to Allan because Allan would have given him one back.

John Bates

He knocked a few rough edges off certain players

Tommy was someone who thought about the game a lot. I don't think we would have won anything without him. First of all he got them fit and I remember what Nigel Stephenson told me. He said that Tommy made training enjoyable.

To start off with they did physical fitness training and then Tommy explained his set moves. Apparently, a lot of the players didn't understand what he was doing at first. He was a very forward-thinking coach. They trained twice a week. Tuesday they concentrated on fitness and Thursday ball handling. Gradually Tommy introduced more set moves. Mick Sullivan coached Dewsbury but he didn't have Tommy's finesse. You can be a good coach/manager, but you have to have some players with ability to work with. Tommy did have some good players and he knocked a few rough edges off certain players. Obviously, it all came together in that Championship final.

Geoff Berry (lifelong fan and former referee)

Tommy Smales' contribution as team coach was a very important factor in Dewsbury's victory over Leeds, but as indicated earlier, there were other reasons why Dewsbury were able to defy the odds, reasons related to individual performances and miscalculations by the opposition.

Everything worked for us

Leeds had a lot of pace with players like Atkinson, Smith, Dyl and Hardisty, so we had to be able to counteract that. Syd Hynes was strong and a good footballer, but we were not worried about his pace. John Clark, who was marking Dyl, could run and he was a great tackler. Greg Ashcroft, on the wing, was as quick as any player on the field so he wasn't worried by Atkinson's pace. He wasn't always great at catching kicks or tackling, but he stuck to his task in that game. On the day, everything worked for us.

It wasn't that Leeds played particularly badly, it was just that players like Joe Whittington played out of their skin and Stevo was too difficult for them to handle. We tackled our hearts out and Leeds were never really able to get going. When they went on a roll, we hit them with another try. They were not able to use the extra pace that they had because we didn't let them. We used the moves that we had developed with Tommy and they worked. We caught them off balance and they weren't able to come back. Tommy Smales deserves a lot of credit for the win. The players did it on the field, but Tommy helped them to do it. He thought about ways to get through defences, or to stop teams getting through our defence.

The previous chairman, Brearley Bailey, who had died, deserves some credit as well because he had built a lot of that team, but unfortunately he wasn't alive when we won the cup.

Nigel Stephenson

Maybe they underestimated us

I don't think that Leeds were overconfident, it was just that we outplayed them. Maybe they underestimated how well we could play. If Hardisty hadn't been sent off, it wouldn't have made much difference. We were in front anyway, when he was sent off. Later on, when I spoke to Alan Hardisty, he said that he didn't think it was a foul, but I said 'C'mon Alan, you nearly killed him.' The stiff arm tackle was on John Bates, who used to run in a very upright manner with his head tilted back a bit, so any high tackle on him would look bad. John and his brother Alan had not played junior rugby like most of the others in the team. They just turned up at Dewsbury and asked if they could have a go at the game. They both ended up playing at international level.

Joe Whittington

Allan had a very good football brain

Allan Agar had played at Featherstone before he came to Dewsbury and he came as a scrum half because we needed a scrum half. I had said 'What about that kid at Featherstone', but I don't know whether that was the reason they got him.

At first, he wasn't very popular with the crowd. Some fans thought he was too slow, but it didn't bother Allan. He said that as long as he was getting paid, he couldn't care less. He said that some fans 'knew nowt about owt and everything about everything else!' Allan had a very good football brain. He had really blossomed as the team gelled together. This was one of the main reasons why we won.

We were all young apart from a couple of the players and we'd been playing together for three years, so it wasn't something that had happened overnight.

Joe Whittington

Tackling was key

I did a lot of tackling during the game, but Mick Stephenson deserved the man of the match. The second try that he scored was great. Leeds just weren't expecting it and that showed just how good he was. He organised the moves on the field and Leeds didn't seem to be able to cope. Tackling is important and so is attitude.

The test is whether you get back up and get ready to go again after you've been walloped in a tackle. There used to be some big blokes who liked to knock smaller players out of the way, but if they got hit with a hard tackle that was them out of the game; they didn't want to know for the rest of the match. As they say in Dewsbury and Batley, they would 'tub it'.

Joe Whittington

We stopped them playing

The Leeds team was filled with star players. I mean there was probably only Graham Eccles and Geoff Clarkson in that team who weren't internationals, either then or later.

On paper, they had a very strong pack with some very good players. Phil Cookson was fast but he wasn't so keen on the rough stuff. He liked to get involved when the hard graft had been done. Anyway, we held them all down with our tackling and didn't give them chance to play.

Greg Ashcroft was our winger opposite Atkinson. He struggled with catching but he was fast and I said to Greg 'don't let him (Atkinson) get away from you' and he didn't. Their wingers didn't score any tries.

Joe Whittington

Very good individual players

We had some very good individual players. Mick Stephenson was very fast for a hooker and Nigel was a good ball distributor with a good sidestep and he was a very reliable goal kicker as well.

We'd been together as a team for quite a while and we had a very solid defence. We worked together, moving up in a line so that there were no gaps and the opponents didn't have much room to move.

Joe Whittington tackled his heart out that day. We made sure that they couldn't get the ball out to the wings because they had two international wingers who were very dangerous. Leeds did not expect to lose but we were better organised than them.

Mick Stephenson scored a great try from a play the ball. He outpaced their defence and they had no answer to that.

John Bates

The Heavy Woollen Victories

The loss to Bradford Northern helped us

In my opinion one of the main reasons why we went on to win the 1973 Championship final was the fact that we had been beaten by Bradford Northern in the Challenge Cup semi-final that same year and we had been favourites to win that game because they were an ageing team.

We didn't do ourselves justice in that game. We weren't as well prepared as we should have been for that game because, as I found out later, a couple of our players had been out drinking late into the night at a disco. When we went back to Dewsbury after that game, it was a wake rather than a celebration.

I said that some players had let us down, but I didn't name them and said that we had had the capability to win so it was embarrassing that we hadn't. We just needed to get on with the next job.

Mike 'Stevo' Stephenson

We didn't argue with the ref

We knew that it would be hard for us to beat Leeds if we let them play like they could. We were a better team than a lot of people thought, but man for man they had a lot more top class players than us.

Nigel Stephenson was a great rugby player and John Clark couldn't half tackle, but their centres were Syd Hynes and Les Dyl, who were very quick. Mick Stephenson was probably as good as anybody Leeds had and he didn't have to do as much tackling as the rest of us in the pack. He was behind the main line to stop anybody who broke through, but that day we hardly missed a tackle and we didn't argue with the ref if we thought that summat was wrong with a decision.

I think that Mick's try in the second half knocked Leeds for six. He could run could Mick and he was strong. When he set off for that try, they just couldn't catch him.

Jeff Grayshon

Positive body language

During the week before the final a lot of supporters met up and we were quietly confident, even though Leeds had a very strong team. I think that the players were confident as well.

Later on, I became a professional referee and got to be a bit of an expert on body language and thinking back I could see that the players' body language was very positive in the play-off matches. It was like they had developed a strong self-belief.

On the day of the final, when they arrived on the bus they were buzzing. They didn't just win, they won well. In some ways the score didn't reflect how well they played. It was a collective effort from the team for all the games leading up to and including the final.

Alan Bates' kicking was outstanding, pinning them down in their own 25. Nigel Stephenson was the same as well. We pinned opponents down and then made something from their mistakes.

Geoff Berry (lifelong Dewsbury fan and former referee)

5.

THE AFTERMATH OF DEWSBURY'S VICTORY

Celebrations

On reflection, given the context of all that has been said, Dewsbury's defeat of Leeds in the 1973 Championship Final was not as surprising as it might at first have seemed. Nonetheless, it was unexpected and was celebrated in suitable fashion.

I'm a beer drinker rather than wine

After the game we all went to a reception at Dewsbury Town Hall. When we came back from Odsal I thought that there might be crowds of people lining the road as we got to Dewsbury, so I was bit disappointed when I didn't see any fans, but then when we got to the Town Hall there was a massive crowd in front of the building, cheering and shouting. We went up onto the balcony with the cup and we thought that we should make sure that we enjoy the occasion.

We had a reception at Crown Flatt, which was brilliant. There were different wines with the food, though I'm a beer drinker rather than wine. Some dignitaries attended as well: the Chief of Police was one of them and the Mayor. The Directors mingled with the crowd but after the food they went into the Board Room and I was invited in there to be congratulated.

I don't know whether the club arranged for the cup to be taken round to local schools and places such as that, like we did at Featherstone in 1967. If they did organise things like that, the Committee never asked me to be involved.

Tommy Smales

Belated celebrations

I didn't get a winner's medal for being the coach of the Championship winning team in 1973. I should have had one, but it never got to me. Eventually, I got a medal and that was because I had mentioned it to Mick Stephenson.

When he was over from Australia he invited me and some of the members of that 1973 team out for a meal in Leeds. We met in Leeds station and had a few beers in the station bar and then went to a restaurant. Whilst we were there, I mentioned that I had never received a medal for the 1973 victory. Stevo was very surprised and said 'I'll rectify that.' A year later, when we met up again Stevo presented me with a medal I should have got in 1973. That's the sort of bloke he is.

Tommy Smales

My wife left my medal on the coach

When we got back to Dewsbury, you can imagine what it was like. There was a massive crowd in front of the Town Hall. It was unbelievable. There were family members and friends in the crowd and there were loads of people waving and cheering. They wanted to see the Championship Cup. A team from a fairly small town, Dewsbury, had beaten a big city team, so people were very excited about what had happened and very proud as well.

We went on to the balcony to show the trophy to the crowd and Stevo made a speech, which was not a problem for him because he loved talking. I think one of the players got engaged after the match. This was my first ever medal and my wife, Angela (she'll complain that I mentioned this), left my medal on the coach that the players' wives had been on. She had picked up John Clark's medal by mistake, so when I asked her if I could look at my medal, she realised that she'd left it on the coach.

Anyway, she got a police escort to the bus depot where they found the medal on the coach and she brought it back. A lot of the team went to 'The Little Saddle' pub in the centre of Dewsbury and everyone was buying them drinks. It was a fantastic time because we were just working class lads playing for a small town team and nobody had expected us to win, so that made it all the more special.

Nigel Stephenson

A pint on the house in every pub

When we were in the bar at Odsal after the match, there were two Featherstone lads in there, Cyril Kellett and Steve Nash, and they raised a glass to us. Back in Dewsbury they had organised a civic reception for us whether we won or not.

When we were on our way back to Dewsbury on the team bus, I was saying that it's going to be embarrassing because there'll be nobody there, but as we got to Batley Carr there were people by a garage and outside some shops and they were clapping. When we got to the centre of Dewsbury and turned left by the Essoldo (cinema) towards the Town Hall, the place was heaving. There is a picture of us getting off the team bus. Unfortunately, there wasn't any alcohol at the reception because the Town Hall didn't have a licence. We went on to the Town Hall balcony and we all held the cup as the crowd was cheering.

There was just some sandwiches, as I remember, at the Town Hall. A little bit of food, but not a lot. I went home, got changed and we met up in the Little Saddle pub in Dewsbury, but I was a Market House man, so I went over the road after a drink in the Saddle.

The day after, I called Stewart Lonergan, who now lives in Spain, and arranged to meet him in the Market House on Sunday lunchtime. When I got there, with my medal in my pocket, Stewart told me to just go back outside and come in again and then he announced me to the whole pub, saying 'Put your hands together for Joe Whittington, who is one of the Dewsbury players who has just won the rugby league Championship.' We went round several pubs in Dewsbury and did the same, and we got a pint each on the house in every pub and in Dewsbury Nash. They(Dewsbury Nash) bought me a carriage clock.

Joe Whittington

Permanent damage to my kidneys

I remember coming back to Dewsbury on the coach, only a couple of hours after the match for a reception at the Town Hall.

We thought that there wouldn't be many people there, but it was heaving and the crowds were cheering. We went on to the Town Hall balcony and held up the trophy and addressed the crowd. I don't remember there being much of a celebration subsequently at the ground, but that might have been because there wasn't much room.

We were able to take the trophy round to various venues and I went to Hanging Heaton cricket club. I got absolutely paralytic because they were filling the Cup with all sorts of different spirits. I'm sure I did some permanent damage to my kidneys as a result of that. I know that when I went to work at the Coal Board the following day, I was in a bit of a state. I drove to work but I must have been well over the limit. The manager at work got someone to drive me home in a Coal Board van.

John Bates

He rolled the base across the polished floor

I got the man of the match award, the Harry Sunderland Trophy, and we were quite some time having photos taken with the trophy. We spent quite a while celebrating in the dressing room, just absorbing what we had done. It was an amazing feeling, especially after the disappointment of losing to Bradford.

When we were on the coach some of the players said let's not rush back, go through the backstreets and take our time. When we turned into the square in front of the Town Hall we couldn't believe it. There was a crowd of six or seven thousand people waiting to greet us.

We went in to the Town Hall and I can remember that Nigel Stephenson had the heavy base of the Championship trophy and he rolled it across the polished floor shouting 'Yeah'. I went out onto the balcony with the trophy and held it up for the crowd.
Mike 'Stevo' Stephenson

We thought there might be a few folk there

After we had been in the bath and got ready we got on the coach and went back to Dewsbury. We thought that there might be a few folk there to cheer us on when we got back, but it was much bigger than that. I couldn't believe it when we got to the square in front of the Town Hall. The streets had been fairly quiet, but when the coach turned the corner into the square, it was packed. I don't think that everybody who was in the square had been to the match, but they had come down to cheer us when we got back. I suppose it was important for the town.

Clubs like Dewsbury and Batley didn't have much money because they hadn't been top teams for a long time, so this was summat big for Dewsbury. I mean, I'm a Birstall lad but I was proud to play for that Dewsbury team. Most of us were local lads. Greg was from Wales but the rest of us were from Dewsbury, Batley and Wakefield area, just ordinary blokes. We went out on to the balcony at the Town Hall and Mick, who was the captain, showed the trophy to the crowd.

Joe Whittington told me that the day after we had won the cup he got a round of applause when he went in to The Market House in Dewsbury to meet his mate. He said that he got a free pint in all the pubs he and his mate went into on the Sunday after the game.
Jeff Grayshon

Select invitations

We went back to Dewsbury and there was a very big crowd, which we weren't expecting in the square in front of the Town Hall. We went into the Town Hall and up onto the balcony and showed the Cup to the crowd, who were cheering.

Later, we had an invite to Hanging Heaton Cricket Club from Trevor Watson, who was a local journalist and had a connection with the cricket club; there were drinks and something to eat. There was a bloke at Hanging Heaton Cricket Club who lived in Mirfield and he had a house there which had a swimming pool. He invited some of the players back to his house, but not all of them, only particular ones.

John Clark

Two Dewsbury fans recall their relatively low key celebrations and express a jaundiced view of some of those who joined the crowd in front of the Town Hall.

We thought it was a night for the players

In those days presentations a the end of the match weren't organised like they are now. We could see the presentation but it wasn't clear because there were people running on the pitch. It took the edge of it a bit because we wanted to be part of the celebrations. Anyway, we waited till the players came up the steps with the trophy, after they had done a lap of honour with the cup. Their faces were unbelievable. You don't forget days like that .

We went back to Dewsbury after the game and to our usual pubs. We went to The Whistler, The Crown, The Royal Oak and then back to The Whistler. We were all from that area, not far from Crown Flatt, so we used those pubs. We didn't go up to the club because we thought that it was a night for the players and we didn't want to spoil that. We got a bollocking later because apparently there were all sorts of hangers on there and not so many committed fans.

We didn't go to the Town Hall because we thought that event was going to take place on Sunday, if Dewsbury had won the cup. Quite a lot of committed fans stayed in Bradford, celebrating in pubs there after the match. I think that there were a lot of glory hunters at the Town Hall as opposed to die-hard supporters. A lot of people claimed to have been at the match who weren't actually there. The crowd would have been double the size if all those who said they were at the match had actually been there.

Geoff Berry (lifelong Dewsbury fan and former referee)

We were celebrating and talking about the game

After the game we went for another drink and then the coaches, apart from those for the players and their families, came straight back to Dewsbury. We went to Eastborough WMC, where we were celebrating and talking about the game. Later the team came to the Town Hall and they were on the balcony, displaying the cup. Of course, there were a lot of people who hadn't been to the game who just turned up in front of the Town Hall and later claimed that they had been to the game. The sort of people who might claim to be supporters and they only turn up at one or two matches and only when they have heard that the team is doing well.

Graham Fisher (lifelong Dewsbury fan)

Optimism and disappointment

The general hope at the club and amongst Dewsbury fans was that this victory would be a platform for continued and sustained success. The Dewsbury Reporter, 25th May, 1973, reported that players and officials at the club were suggesting that this was just the start. Tommy Smales was quoted as saying "It will be Wembley next year."

As we shall see, Tommy Smales certainly had plans to strengthen the Dewsbury team and the 1973/74 season was a relatively successful one for the club, but in retrospect the Championship victory was the high watermark for Dewsbury RLFC post-World War Two. For individual players whose reputations had been enhanced by Dewsbury's successful Championship campaign, the victory opened up opportunities that might not otherwise have been available. For others, like Joe Whittington who suffered disappointment in the aftermath of the Championship final victory, the experience of playing rugby league has provided unforgettable memories.

I had big plans for the team

I had big plans for the team after this victory. I wanted to strengthen the team because one or two were coming towards the end of their playing careers, so I needed suitable replacements. The club sold Mick Stephenson to Penrith for a big transfer fee and I expected that I would be able to use some of that money to strengthen the team. However, I became disillusioned because I wasn't told how much the club had received for Mick and it was made clear to me that the money was not available to buy new players.

The committee members said that I had done very well with the existing players, but they didn't seem to realise that they wouldn't always be there. The transfer fee was put in the bank so that it could generate interest which would help with the day to day running of the club.

I had drawn up a five-year plan which is the sort of thing I had come across at work, but the committee members were not interested in that sort of thing.

I was very disappointed with the lack of ambition. I think that some of the committee members were only interested in being members of the committee (board of directors) in order to have a bit of prestige locally; maybe to give a boost to their own small businesses. The idea of a five-year plan was beyond them.

They didn't interfere much with team selection, they generally left that to me, but I couldn't build anything if I didn't have some resources. At one point I suggested that, as a way of showing their commitment to the club, each of the directors should put in a £1000 if they didn't want to use the money from Mick Stephenson's transfer fee and then we could make some progress. Nothing came of that.

I had nearly four years at Dewsbury and I thought that I improved the team a lot, but within a year of winning the

Championship I couldn't see a way of making any more progress because the ambition wasn't there, so I left. I didn't even receive a letter of thanks.

Tommy Smales

I thought that they didn't know how to handle a successful team

The saddest part of it all was that Stevo was sold to Penrith in Australia. We thought that Dewsbury was going to keep on improving, but the team broke up fairly quickly after that Championship final win.

It didn't happen straight away because we did well for a couple of years, beating a lot of strong teams and finishing high up in the league. I thought that the club committee didn't know how to handle such a successful team. Of course, the players wanted more money and if Dewsbury wouldn't pay them more and other clubs would, they moved on. Allan Agar and John Bates left, Jeff Grayshon went and by 1978 I had become disillusioned with the club. I requested a transfer and then withdrew it but Leeds came in for me, wanting me to play at fullback, but I didn't fancy that as I lacked the pace for that position, so when Bradford, where Peter Fox was the coach, approached me I signed for them and stayed there three years.

That win in the final meant that my name became known in rugby league circles. I was working as a joiner at ICI, but if I had a bad game they would let me know at work. They always brought me down to earth, which was good. The fact that I'd played in the Championship final and had scored 16 points in the game was no big deal to them.

I used to sign a lot of autographs for little lads who came to watch matches and that was not something that I imagined I would be doing when I started playing. I remember that, as local celebrities, me and Stevo were there for the opening of a TV shop in Dewsbury and I did a bit of talking on Radio Leeds. I took the Cup to an assembly at my old school and I will never forget that match with my hometown club. It meant more than anything I did later on in my career, even with Bradford. I'm still recognised when I'm out and about in Dewsbury, by older fans because the younger ones haven't any idea about that game.

Nigel Stephenson

I didn't know it was my last game for Dewsbury

The final was my last game for Dewsbury, but I didn't know that at the time. Three months later I was off to Penrith in Australia.

They approached me when I was working in Harrogate. I got a phone call from someone with an Australian accent who arranged to meet me at the Dragonara Hotel in Leeds. He said that Penrith were the wooden spooners, so at that time they were not a top team. He said that they had watched video clips of me and they wanted me to play for Penrith. My father-in-law, Roland Tolson, was a director at Dewsbury and of course he wasn't keen for his daughter to go to Australia but Penrith agreed to pay what Dewsbury asked for, so they released me.

Before I went to Australia, Dewsbury played an Australian touring team and the club asked me to kick off. I got some terrible abuse from a minority of fans who said I was a traitor. They were booing me and spitting at me. It was upsetting because I had been at Dewsbury for about nine years and I was going to Australia for a better life for me and my family. I earned more in one game for Penrith than in a whole year at Dewsbury. I certainly didn't think that I had let the club down. I'd helped to improve the team.

The club didn't use the money they got for me to strengthen the team, so that Championship win wasn't a platform for future success. Anyway, I had a good career in Australia and then a long career in the media, which I always wanted to get involved in.

Mike 'Stevo' Stephenson

Disappointment and reconciliation

The first match next season was against Featherstone, the Challenge Cup holders, at home and the TV cameras were there. The Challenge Cup was on display and we walloped them.

Then, I ended up having a major falling out over the Australia game. I was dropped and that shattered me because I didn't understand why. I had been suspended for one match and there had been a midweek match before the Australia game, so I could have played. I just didn't want to play after that. I had a bit of a beef with Tommy Smales because he had me in the A team and I just wasn't happy. Eventually Alan Hardisty came and begged me to come back.

He came to the house and said that he knew my game and I should come back to the team. Anyway, I went back training Tuesday and Thursday and I played a match for the A team and played very well. They said that they had some injuries, so I would be playing for the first team against Leeds at the weekend, on New Year's Day which was a bank holiday for the first time. Well, I wasn't happy about that so said 'I'm injured too!' and stopped playing again.

Towards the back end of 1974, Dewsbury rang me up and said that they were really struggling and that they could pick me up at 11:00am on Long Causeway in Dewsbury. When I got on the bus there was only one person on it that I knew, John Frain.

It was the A team and when I asked who we were playing, they said Hull at Hull. John Maloney played that day for Hull and he must have mentioned me when they had their team talk before the game because the first time I was tackled I went up in the air. After the game, John Maloney told me that on that performance, I should soon be back in the first team.

In 1977, at the Player of the Year Dinner, the club chairman came up to me and asked me how many games I'd played for Dewsbury and how many tries I'd scored. I said about 300 games and not many tries, but they were all good 'uns.

I wasn't going to stay for the meal, but the chairman insisted that I sit on the top table. Later, the chairman announced that the player whose career people had come to celebrate had played 300 games for Dewsbury etc. I wasn't forewarned about this, so it was a surprise. I was inducted into the Hall of Fame.

Joe Whittington

Great memories of playing rugby league

Looking back, I've got some great memories of playing rugby league. That Championship final win was very special.

I remember when I played my first game for Dewsbury first team and Dick Lowe, who was my favourite player at Dewsbury, talked to me in the tunnel, giving advice and encouraging me. I came on in the second half and I saw this figure coming towards me and he hit me like an express train. It was Neil Fox I'd tackled. He said to me 'OK, young'un?' I almost said 'I'm OK Mr Fox!'

There were some tough men playing then.

On one occasion Jeff Grayshon was at a British Lions dinner, sitting next to Eric Chisnall, and Eric Chisnall said to Jeff, 'You played for Dewsbury didn't you?' When Jeff said that he had played for Dewsbury, Eric Chisnall said 'Have you seen anything of that bastard Whittington?' Jeff said 'He's my best mate.'

Once when we had played St Helens in a quarter final and we lost 6-4, Eric was going around dishing it out and he caught me on the nose with his elbow in a tackle and there was blood everywhere. Later on, Eric came in to tackle me again and I ducked but he hit me again in the nose with his forearm and my nose just disintegrated. So, when I went with John Maloney to the rugby league centenary celebrations at Huddersfield in 1995, I saw Eric. I covered my name tag as I approached him and asked him how he was and he said he was doing ok. He didn't realise who I was until I uncovered the name tag and then his face fell. He held his arm out and said 'Look at this.'

There were two scars on his forearm, one on the front and one on the back. The surgeons had had to open it up from both sides for an operation on his arm. He said the damage had been done when he was tackling me. I saw him again with his brother in Blackpool and I said 'Hey up Eric, how are you doing?' and he said 'My wife hates you. Every time my arm hurts and I am complaining about it, she curses you.' Then he said 'Wife's coming and my arm's been hurting today, so you'd best be off!' They're all good memories.

Joe Whittington

The Heavy Woollen Victories

I won the Challenge Cup with Hull KR

The win in the final got us noticed because nobody had expected us to win. I went on to play at Hull KR. I played at scrum half, which is the position I had played at Featherstone, but when I went to Dewsbury they already had a scrum half so I played stand-off there.

I always preferred scrum half and, of course, at Hull KR they had a world class stand-off, Roger Millward. I won the Challenge Cup with Hull KR in 1980, when we beat Hull. I was playing behind an international pack at Hull KR so that made my life a bit easier than normal. Dewsbury had a good pack as well. Three of them became internationals.

Allan Agar

The victory in the final gave my career a boost

The year after the final I was picked to tour Australia, along with Allan. I played a few matches but then I got injured at Tamworth and had to come home, along with John Atkinson who had also been injured. That victory in the final had given my career a boost, but I got a bad head injury in 1975 and I decided to bail out. I was 32 and I'd had a good run.

I played for Yorkshire a few times. On one occasion I was on holiday in Bournemouth and got a phone call from the chairman of Yorkshire Rugby League. He said that I was needed for a game, so I drove up to Keighley, played in the match, and then drove back down to Bournemouth.

I did a bit of coaching after I'd retired but I decided that it wasn't for me. Anyway, I was running a business so didn't have much time.

John Bates

Disappointment that Dewsbury didn't do even better

I allus thought that Dewsbury should have been able to use that win to go on and do even better, but we didn't. We didn't do too badly the following season. I think that we finished a bit higher up the table. (1973/74 there were two divisions and Dewsbury finished 6th in the top division, effectively two places higher than in the previous season). We had lost our best player. Mick Stephenson was signed by Penrith more or less straight after we had beaten Leeds.

I didn't really know 'owt about what was going on behind the scene, but I could guess that Tommy wasn't getting much money from the directors to strengthen the team. Trevor Lowe retired and I think that Greg Ashcroft had to pack in playing because of injury. Eventually, both me and Nigel [Stephenson] went to play for Bradford and John Bates got injured while he was on tour in Australia. I'll never forget that match though.

Jeff Grayshon

Short-lived success

Because we'd won the Championship in 1973, we were given a game against the Aussie touring team next season. Mick Stephenson had gone to Penrith of course, so he wasn't playing, but I remember that Arthur Beetson was in the Australian team and Steve Atkins fouled him so Beetson punched him in the head in the scrum and knocked him out of the pack. We didn't do too badly against them and had a decent season, but it was all downhill from there.

John Clark

He had damaged the scaphoid bone in his hand

Greg went back to Wales in 1975, I think. He had damaged the scaphoid bone in his hand in training and that ended his playing career. He trained with Cardiff Blue Dragons but because of his injury he wasn't able to play any matches for them.

It also affected his job, because for the last 15 years or so he wasn't able to do much tool work, but we'd set up a small building contractor's business and we employed 10 locals, doing work for the local authority. We got quite big contracts for a small firm.

He did some coaching of two amateur rugby league teams, Valley Cougars and Blackwood Bulldogs. He did two separate spells at

Valley Cougars. He was the first head coach at Blackwood in 2006 and then at Valley Cougars he was with Adrian Barwood, who had played at Wakefield Trinity, and in 2008 they won the Welsh Grand Final. They beat Blackwood Bulldogs in Bridgend (26-12).

There were a few players who went on to play for Wales at rugby league, like Steve Parry and Paul Emanuelli. They said that they learned a lot from Greg. Valley Cougars played at Nelson and Treharris. They're still playing, but they might have moved.

Greg loved doing the coaching. He went on a number of coaching courses and he used to organise training a couple of times a week. Gerwyn Price, 'The Iceman', the World Darts' Champion, played rugby league at Blackwood.

Diane Ashcroft (Greg Ashcroft's widow)

I don't think we spent the money wisely

It was a bit of a damp squib at the end of the season because there were rumours that Stevo was leaving. He was sold to Penrith for £20k, which was a lot of money at the time. People were disappointed, but it was a chance for him to develop his career. It did take the edge off winning the Championship; it was a bit of a downer. We got Keith Voyce and he wasn't bad, but he was never going to be a full replacement for Stevo. He was a better ball striker in the scrum but he was not as agile in the loose, but it was an impossible task to fill Stevo's boots.

The following season we played quite well, but we were not consistent. I think that we beat Wigan in the first game of the season and then we lost to Warrington in the Challenge Cup semi-final. I don't think that we spent the money wisely. We bought fringe players instead of well-known names and it just didn't work.

When a player was bought, we were saying who's that, we haven't heard of him. I don't know for certain but I don't think that Tommy Smales had much say over who was bought. We had an injury free season, but we didn't have much strength in depth. It seemed that we bought some players just for the sake of it and it didn't work. From the end of 1974 things started to decline and of course now, because of Super League , we'll never go back to where we were. Dewsbury just hasn't got the money. In the Championship the stronger clubs get stronger and the weaker clubs weaker.

Two to three years after the Championship final win spectators were becoming distraught because we were losing key players and the team was breaking up. The replacements would never have got into that 1973 team. Obviously, I carried on supporting them, but it was very disappointing after we had done so well. Some things were unavoidable, like John Bates getting injured on tour. Those things happen and you have to accept injuries, but not losing star players and replacing them with numpties.

Geoff Berry (lifelong Dewsbury fan and former referee)

You start to lose your top players to wealthier clubs

It was a bit disappointing because I thought that the team would be going places after this performance. They had a great team spirit and they were mostly local lads who were not big names at the time.

Of course, bigger clubs eventually came in and they raided the players. Stevo was the first to go and I think that he was sold to Penrith for a record fee for a hooker. You can't blame him for taking up the offer. Nigel Stephenson and Jeff Grayshon went later, so the team started to break up. It was great that they won the Championship but the knock-on effect for clubs like Dewsbury is that you start to lose your top players to wealthier clubs.

It's still happening today, If you are a small club and you do very well, then bigger clubs will take your best players and you can't blame the players for leaving for more money or a bigger challenge.

Graham Fisher (lifelong Dewsbury fan)

A fitting epitaph

There should be a film made about Dewsbury's victory. There's a film just been made about the Grand National Winner that was kept on an allotment in Blackwood and owned by a group of locals.

Diane Ashcroft (Greg Ashcroft's widow)

PART 2

BATLEY RLFC 2010 – NORTHERN RAIL CUP WINNERS

1.

THE ROAD TO
BLACKPOOL

BY 2010, THE YEAR in which Batley won the Northern Rail Cup, the rugby league landscape had changed considerably since Dewsbury's Championship victory in 1973.

The establishment of Super League and full-time professional teams in 1996 meant that a Grand Final victory, the modern equivalent of the Championship final, was no longer a possibility for semi-professional teams like Batley and Dewsbury.

In 2010, The Northern Rail Cup Final was the Championship final for the teams in the tier below Super League.

Moreover, post-1996 a Wembley Challenge Cup final appearance has been beyond a Championship club, so for a team like Batley, inaugural winners of the Challenge Cup, the Northern Rail Cup final was the equivalent.

It was eighty-six years since Batley had won a major trophy, so the club and the local community were hungry for success.

The Batley team that beat Widnes, 25-24, in the Northern Rail Cup Final at Blackpool on Sunday 18th July, 2010 was as follows: Jonny Campbell; Lee Greenwood, Mark Toohey, Danny Maun, Alex Brown; Paul Handforth, Gareth Moore; Byron Smith, Kris Lythe, Sean Hesketh, Jason Walton, John Gallagher, Ash Lindsay. Substitutes: Mick Govin, Tommy Gallagher, Dave Toothill, James Martin.

Local lads

The team had a really good coach, Karl Harrison, and most of the members of the team were local lads. I think that they all came from no further than 10 miles from Batley's ground, so they were a close-knit team with a very good spirit. That makes a lot of difference.

Richard Drake (lifelong Batley fan)

A speculative approach

Karl Harrison had come to the club as coach midway through the 2009 season, when we were struggling to avoid relegation and then he coached us to the Northern Rail Cup win just over a year later.

We'd also managed to get Tiger Handforth from Doncaster and he was a crucial player. That was a stroke of luck because Doncaster were in financial difficulties and they had to sell players, otherwise we might not have been able to get Tiger. Karl had been out of the game as well and I think that he had become a bit disillusioned after his experience at Salford, but it was a speculative approach when we contacted him.

I think that I had checked with Paul Harrison that there was a possibility that his brother would agree to join us as coach, that he would be interested in the job. Gary Thornton had decided to step down and we'd had a meeting about who we could get to replace him. We contacted Karl and suggested that he should come up to the club for a chat and when he did he immediately agreed to our offer. We lost the first game with Karl as the coach. I think it was at Barrow and I jokingly said to him: "I thought you knew what you were doing!" I was wondering whether we had made the wrong decision, but Karl got them working very well together. He moulded them into a tight unit. In addition to Tiger Handforth, who was the trigger to get us playing well, we had Paddy Hesketh, who was back to his best when he came back to Batley.

Kevin Nicholas (Chairman, Batley RLFC)

We'd had to struggle

I'd come to Batley from Doncaster because they were in a bit of financial trouble and what people forget is that we had been in danger of relegation the season before we won the Northern Rail Cup. That experience did us a lot of good, because we had to struggle and that meant that we all had to work together and you can't overestimate how important that is.

Paul Handforth

They turned their noses up at us

Some of our players had been at Super League teams and others were like me, who hadn't been at a Super League club. Some of the bigger Championship clubs with better finance than Batley sort of turned their noses up at us. It was a case of who are these vagabonds? Once we got involved with the rough and tumble of the top six, we showed what we could do.

I hadn't played with any of the team members but I knew Tommy Gallagher personally. There were a lot of locals in the team, which is what Karl wanted and it helped bring the team together. They were a great bunch of lads and I'm still in touch with several, even though your lives go in different directions when you've finished playing.

Kris Lythe

He got his compass out

Karl Harrison made a big thing about having a team consisting of locals, players who were from Batley or not far from Batley, from

West Yorkshire. I think he got his compass out and measured the distance. Mick Govin was the exception, because he was from Leigh.

It made sense because it fed into the team spirit and it meant that it was easier for players to get to training sessions. It might not be that far to travel from places like Oldham and Rochdale but you've got to get across the Pennines and in winter and spring that can be a problem.

Lee Greenwood

A number of different positions

I had been at Batley since I was 15 and for some of the time we had struggled to stay up. I broke my thumb in four places on one occasion and that put me out for the rest of the season.

Once Karl came as coach, he made it clear that he wanted to win the Northern Rail Cup. I had the best pre-season then, no injuries, so I was in good condition for the season. I played in a number of different positions, as a utility player, so I wasn't certain that I would be in the team for the cup run. Josh Griffin was on loan and he was a centre and playing well. As it happened, Josh was not eligible for the Northern Rail Cup matches, so that gave me the chance.

Mark Toohey

They had a point to prove

Batley didn't have a lot of money, so players had to want to play for the team because they couldn't be doing it just for that. Sometimes it was players who had been at other clubs that didn't want them, so they had a point to prove.

I'd been at Castleford and Featherstone and then York. Karl Harrison was interested in me and I wanted to play for him because he had been a prop and I thought I could learn something from him. He told me that he couldn't pay anything other than match terms.

Sean Hesketh

The Northern Rail Cup competition commenced at the end of January 2010 with the Championship clubs divided into two pools, with ten teams in each. Every team then played four matches within their pool, at the end of which the pool stage was completed.

The top four teams from each of the two pools then progressed into an open draw for the quarter finals, the winners of which entered an open draw for the semi-finals, with the final scheduled to take place at Bloomfield Road, Blackpool, at 4:00 pm on the 18th July 2010. At no stage in this competition was the Batley team defeated, dropping only one point in the pool stage of the competition as a result of a draw with Widnes, their subsequent opponents in the dramatic 2010 Northern Rail Cup final.

In the early stages of the competition, Batley had to play three games in eight days as a result of the postponement of their first-round match against Whitehaven. Consequently, they faced Widnes at home on the 7th February 2010 and then had to travel to play Whitehaven on the 10th February in a mid-week game before facing Swinton at The Mount on the 14th February.

The Batley News, *11th February, 2010, covered Batley's 30-30 draw with Widnes and according to Malcolm Haig's report Batley stunned the home supporters with "spectacular" rugby, scoring four tries in the first-half, the Widnes response acting only as a catalyst for Batley to press on. It was an eighty-yard move which led to Jonny Campbell's try which came after Preece had scored by finishing off a move which had incorporated runs by Hesketh, Byron Smith and Kris Lythe. Preece "raced ahead, punted up-field and outpaced defenders to score in the corner."*

In the same edition of the Batley News, *Karl Harrison told Trevor Watson that the draw felt like a defeat, adding "We need to learn how to defend our goal line. Widnes scored all their tries from close to our line. That is something we haven't been able to fully work on because of the weather and in that respect we are behind in our preparations." This was clearly a priority for the coach, who also mentioned that he had been speaking to Huddersfield about Alex Brown and dual registration, an arrangement which turned out to be very important for Batley. The re-arranged fixture against Whitehaven, which was scheduled for the evening, almost did not go ahead.*

It shouldn't really have been played

I can remember one particular game between Whitehaven and Batley which had been re-arranged because the ground was too hard. Anyway, it was re-arranged as an evening match and of course no regard had been taken of the fact that the temperature would drop in the evening, so if it was a cold day, the likelihood was that the ground would be too hard by kick-off time.

In fact, the re-arranged match shoudn't really have been played because of the frost but Rhino (Karl Harrison) said to me that if I thought that Batley were coming all the way up to Whitehaven and not playing, I had another thing coming, so we played and it was a high scoring match which Batley won (26-34).

Robert Hicks (referee)

It was a good old-fashioned game

It's true, when we played Whitehaven in the postponed game the pitch wasn't really fit for playing on because it was an evening match and the temperature had dropped. I told him that we hadn't come all the way up to Whitehaven to not play a match. It was a good old-fashioned game of rugby league. Some parts of the pitch were frozen and some parts were boggy, but we managed to get through it.

Karl Harrison

Freezing cold

I went to some of the early rounds of the competition. I remember driving over from Marske to Whitehaven for a mid-week game in the evening. I think it was in February. Was freezing cold and there was only one man and his dog there. On the terrace where I was there were only about three other spectators.

John McVeigh (fan)

DEWSBURY—R.L. CHAMPIONSHIP WINNERS

Dewsbury fans get in on the act on the day the championship is won.

The original caption says it all, *above*.
Nigel Stephenson and Jeff Grayshon show off the trophy

John Roe collection

Dewsbury take title and show Leeds flaws

Dewsbury 22, Leeds 13

A couple of *Yorkshire Post* headlines from the time

John Roe collection

Dewsbury defence holds out

Warrington 7, Dewsbury 12

Dewsbury's triumphant 1973 squad lines up for a photograph

John Roe collection

Left: Stevo holds the trophy aloft in a now famous image

A newspaper diagram, *right*, of a vital Dewsbury set move during the Championship final
John Roe collection

Dewsbury's 50th anniversary reunion on 19 May 2023. *Left to right*: Mike Stephenson, Trevor Lowe, John Bates, Nigel Stephenson, Steve Lee, Alan Bates, Allan Agar, Tommy Smales   *John Roe*

Alex Brown looks relieved, *left*, after his superb try gets the green light
John Roe collection

Batley Bulldogs celebrate winning the Northern Rail Cup

John Roe collection

Byron Smith in typically hard-running action against Widnes, who on the day were favourites
John Roe collection

Jubilant Batley supporters enjoy all the fun of the seaside on the bus *John Roe collection*

Darren Rhodes in his green mankini
John Roe collection

Jean Dennis and grandson, *above*, at the Northern Rail Cup Final
John Roe collection

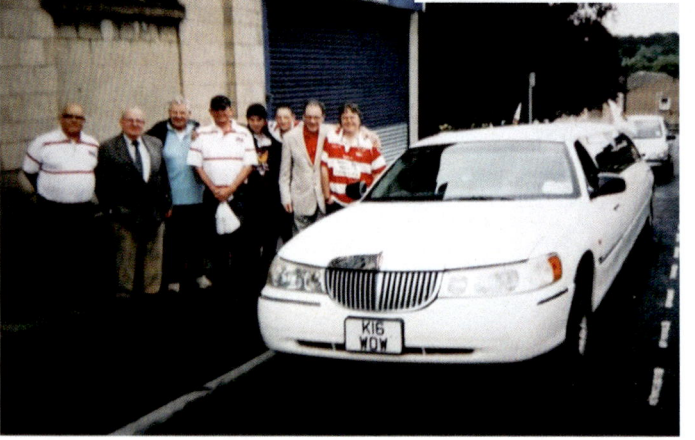

John Atkins and friends ready to go to Blackpool
John Roe collection

This midweek game against Whitehaven was a hard-fought win for Batley, who scored a try in the last four minutes in a game in which the score at one point was 26-26.

According to Malcolm Haigh, in the Batley News, *18th February, 2010, "Batley dug deep and near the end the hosts failed to clear their line after a Handforth drop goal went wide. Sean Hesketh was on hand to plunge over for a try which Moore improved…"*

In the same edition of the Batley News, *Malcolm Haigh reported on Batley's victory against Swinton, a game in which Batley scored six second-half tries down the slope. This reinforces the local view that it is much better for Batley to play downhill in the second half because it's easier to gather momentum when running with the ball. However, an alternative view is that when the team is playing downhill in the second half, defending can be more tiring because the defending team must retreat uphill. According to Malcolm Haigh "The season's positional switch of former fullback Ian Preece, and winger Jonny Campbell continued to delight. Preece not only stiffened the wingside defence – critical against Holroyd's kicks to the corner – but showed his attacking ability by racing in for a hat-trick of tries.*

It is hoped that after these impressive cup games the number of spectators will increase. It was something of a slight on the team that, following a draw with Widnes and victory at Whitehaven, only 509 could be bothered to cheer them on."

This final sentence highlights what has, in recent years, been a perennial problem for Batley and one which their Northern Rail Cup victory has failed to resolve.

In their match against Gateshead on 17th March, 2010, Batley notched up a record score as they thrashed the opposition 100-4. Gareth Moore kicked sixteen goals from seventeen attempts, in addition to scoring two tries for a record forty points. According to the report in the Batley News, *25th March, 2010, Batley demonstrated a killer instinct in so far as they did not ease off in the second-half despite leading 42-4 at the interval. The report said that: "The main feature of the second half was that the Batley players, well aware that they were far superior, did not indulge themselves with individual efforts to score but concentrated on playing as a team and developing their attacking play..."*

Batley overcame Sheffield by 26-16 in their quarter-final tie at The Mount. Writing in the Batley News, *10th June, 2010, Malcolm Haigh claimed that "Batley blasted their way into the semi-final of the Northern Rail Cup with a sizzling session of three tries in seven minutes just before the break."*

Apparently, it was more difficult for Batley in the second half, when Sheffield were playing downhill, but their performance was boosted by Brown's presence. Haigh added that "Batley's never-say-die spirit, epitomised by Lythe, Lindsay, Danny Maun and Hesketh, saw them through in the end."

The semi-final against Leigh

When Batley were drawn against Leigh in the semi-final of the Northern Rail Cup, a game that was to be played on Leigh's home turf, few gave them a chance of winning. In the end, Batley achieved a stunning victory, winning by twenty- five points to four. What is interesting, perhaps, are the slightly different ways in which Karl Harrison's pre-match talk is remembered by the players.

They were shell-shocked

When we played in the semi-final, nobody gave us a chance, but I reckon that it was our best performance that season. Karl Harrison was brilliant as a coach.

He wanted us to be tough and he taught us how to defend, which is what we did in that semi-final against Leigh. We were playing how Karl wanted us to play and I think that it came as a shock to Leigh. They were not expecting us to play like we did and I think that there is still some resentment at Leigh that we beat them, because they were the favourites to win the Cup.

They were shell-shocked because they felt that it was their year. I think that it was my best performance ever for Batley. I think that the team only missed about four tackles during the whole game.

They had a lot of very good players in their team and they had some dual-reg players. That win gave me a real boost because it showed me that I could compete with the best players in our league.

Danny Maun

No way we were going to be beaten

When we played in the semi-final, nobody gave us a chance, but I reckon that it was our best performance that season. Karl Harrison was brilliant as a coach. He wanted us to be tough and he taught us how to defend, which is what we did in that semi-final against Leigh.

We were playing how Karl wanted us to play and I think that it came as a shock to Leigh. They were not expecting us to play like we did and I think that there is still some resentment at Leigh that we beat them, because they were the favourites to win the Cup.

Paul Handforth

You develop the habit of winning

I think that the semi-final against Leigh was our best game in terms of the rugby that we played.

Karl Harrison just came into the dressing room and opened his notebook and said "Just win." Then he closed it and walked out of the dressing room. That did the trick. We were all pumped up and ready to get stuck in. You could feel the atmosphere in the room after he had said that.

It had been building from the previous year. We'd been in difficulty and then at the back end of the year we'd had a few good wins and the team just clicked. It's like they say: you develop the habit of winning.

I think that we'd beaten Leigh earlier in the season. They'd had a few injuries, but they had a strong squad. It was fantastic to be around the club and to always be considered the underdogs, because that just spurred us on.

Kris Lythe

The Heavy Woollen Victories

I put my shoulder out

The semi-final against Leigh was a really tough game and I put my shoulder out during that game and had to come off. I was desperate to get back on the field because I wanted to play in the final.

They said that I might need an operation to fix it properly, but I was determined to play in the final. I went back to Huddersfield and they said that I would be ok with it bandaged up if I could bench press a certain weight, which I did. In the end I didn't have an operation, but now if I play, I have to warm it up a bit.

Alex Brown

None of the players were shocked

You've probably heard about Karl's team talk before the semi against Leigh. He just came in and sat down on a stool or the upturned ice bucket and said "Batley, Northern Rail Cup winners 2010" and then went out of the dressing room. The key thing I remember about that is that none of the players were shocked. They just thought "yeah, that's right and that's what we're going to do." Karl had got us to that stage and our mentality was that Leigh were not going to beat us.

I think that I got held up on the line a couple of times and could have ended up scoring, but the main thing I remember is how well we defended. We didn't allow Leigh to get going. We were all playing for each other and that was a marker for where we were as a team by then. We squeezed them out of the game and there was nothing they could do about it because in the end we beat them easily. We had a great team spirit and that was something which took Leigh by surprise. I'd never known anything like it and that sort of thing is hard to replicate. We had a mindset in that game that we were not going to let Leigh score. Obviously, you can't do that every week and they did score, but only once and they eventually became frustrated. That also might have been because they were expecting to win and were surprised with what they came up against. We broke their spirit so that in the end they believed they couldn't win.

Lee Greenwood

I took some tramadol

Leigh were red hot favourites to win the semi-final, especially as it was on their home ground, but it put the pressure on them because expectations were high. Apart from Karl and the team, nobody expected us to win. I played in the centre and I had a rotator cuff injury. I took some tramadol and when we came in for half time I was shaking. Rachel, the physio, asked me what I had taken and when I told her she said "You silly get!" I'd never used it before and I didn't realise how strong it was. As a result, the game was a bit of a blur, but I can remember that we defended really well and we made sure that their key players, like Robbie Paul, never really got going.

I think that it was a big surprise for them, the way we played, although we had given them a decent game previously. They put a lot of pressure on us in the first part of the game, but we didn't buckle and I think that instead of wearing us down it wore them down and they began to wonder what they would have to do to beat us. In the end, we won convincingly and I think that they only managed one try. In the last part of the game we started to move the ball about and you could see that they were gone. It was our defence that won us the game, because they couldn't break us down and they began to lose heart.

When the game was over everyone was on a massive high and that win gave us a lot of belief. We'd managed to reach a major final and we beaten the favourites. We were all buzzing and we thought that we could do the same in the final. Why not, we'd beaten Leigh at their ground.

Mark Toohey

We stifled them

When we played Leigh in the semi-final we knew that we were underdogs. Most of the rugby league fraternity thought that we didn't have a hope. In the end, it wasn't a close game. We played very well and we executed the plan. There is no doubt that they were well beaten and I think that it was the way in which we beat them that shocked people. We stifled them and didn't give them a chance to get going. We played as a tight knit team and we wanted to work for each other. On paper, Leigh were the better team and it's possible that they thought that the game was going to be a formality. I think that the crucial part of our win that day was the defence.

The fact that they tried to break us down but couldn't do it knocked the stuffing out of them. They were used to running over teams and when they couldn't do that, didn't know what to do.

Byron Smith

We just took it all in

In some ways the semi-final against Leigh was more important than the final because they were still a big club and they were very strong favourites. I mean they had some very good individual players and nobody thought that Batley was going to beat them. I just remember Karl Harrison's team talk before the match. We were all waiting patiently, so it was quite dramatic. He said 'I've only written one thing down. Batley Northern Rail Cup winners 2010.' Then he closed his book and that was it. That geed everyone up and we just cracked on. Everyone was punching the walls. Nobody had given us a shout of winning, but his message worked. It took a lot of effort and we were knackered at the end of the game from both the effort and the emotion but the adrenalin was pumping and we knew that we could do it. We just took it all in and we were ready to go. Karl had faith in us to do the job and we believed that we could do it.

It was a really tough match because Leigh were a good side and we knew that it would be a slog and that we would have to get on top of them and not give them easy chances. That's just how it was at first and we tackled them out of it, which I guess is something that they weren't expecting. We knew that we had to be full on all the time because they had individuals who could do some damage. We kept our concentration and effort at a very high level for the whole match and it paid off. We reaped the benefit of that in the second half and we pulled away from them. It wasn't just that we managed to shut them out. We played well and we scored some good tries. I scored a try right in front of the Batley fans because we were playing towards their end in the second half and that was a big help.

Sean Hesketh

I'm surprised that the score was 25-4

The semi-final against Leigh was a really tough game. We had to do a lot of defending because they were a good team. I remember that we did a lot of defending on our line and then eventually we got control. I thought that we were outstanding that day.

Karl put a lot of emphasis on defence; that was his approach. He encouraged us to enjoy defending and as a result we got more and more confident. Leigh had a good team and that win gave us a lot of confidence. We knew that we could win the final. Karl got people believing that we could beat any team in the Championship. He helped to build a great team spirit.

I'm surprised that we beat Leigh by 25 -4 because my memories of the game are mainly that we were keeping them out. I guess what happened is that as the game went on and they couldn't get through, our confidence grew and they faded. They had some big names, like Robbie Paul, but they couldn't break us down and we just piled it on them in the last fifteen minutes or so.

Normally, Karl's team talk before a game normally lasted five or ten minutes, but in this case he said something like "just win the fucking game", all we needed. He saw how focused we were.

John Gallagher

It was a blood bath

I think that I didn't miss a match that season. Leigh were the strong favourites to win the semi-final and it was a blood bath, a really hard game, extremely physical and a game in which we had to do a lot of defending. I remember that three or four players from Leigh had to leave the field and that made it a bit easier for Batley. Jonny Campbell suffered a head injury, but he carried on. These days he would probably have had to go off and might not have been able to return. They bombed a few tries, but we felt that we could have beaten any side in the Championship that day, we were so revved up. Karl's approach was that defence wins you the games. If you keep the other team out and frustrate them, you'll get your chances to score and you just need to do the simple things very well.

On paper, Leigh had a much stronger team and the match was at their ground, so to beat them there felt like we had won a final and that gave us the belief and motivation for the final.

Ash Lindsay

One of the bravest performances I can remember

When we played Leigh in the semi-final, they were allegedly the favourites to win the trophy, but we were confident that we could beat them.

I think that I gave the shortest team talk ever before that game. Normally, I might have focused on some technical details about our strategy, but I just said "Sit down lads'" and then "Batley, Northern Rail Cup winners 2010" and then I walked out. Batley's performance in that game was one of the bravest performances from a team that I can remember.

We were under the pump for a large part of the game, but we were so dogged and didn't buckle. We stuck to the plan and, in the end, we were comfortable winners. It was on TV and that set us up nicely for the final. We were pretty confident that we could beat Widnes because we had beaten them before. I was pleased that we were seen as the underdogs, because that took the pressure off us and we didn't feel as though we were the underdogs. We knew that we could win.

Karl Harrison

Karl Harrison's truncated team-talk clearly did the trick for his players, but Batley fans, whilst delighted with the result had not all been so confident about their team's chances of defeating Leigh.

One game too many

I wasn't able to go to the semi-final because it was a mid-week game and I was working. I thought that this match would be one game too many for Batley, especially as it was at Leigh. But they played out of their skin and it was a shock because we beat them at their own ground, although Leigh had been playing well up to then. We beat them easily.

John McGowan (fan and ex-Batley player)

The noise was fantastic

In the first place it was a big surprise that Batley had got so far in the competition when they got to the semi-final and we didn't expect to beat Leigh. Robbie Paul was playing for them. He had come back from an injury and he didn't seem to be fully match fit. He was limping around and trying to organise their game plan, but we outperformed them and we outshouted them. The noise was fantastic even though they had stuck us in a corner of the stand, out of the way. We were walking up and down singing "We're on our way to Blackpool!" It wasn't even close at the finish. I think we won by about twenty points(Batley won 25 – 4) . There were rumours that Leigh had already booked coaches to travel to Blackpool, which was a bit disrespectful if you ask me.

Billy Lonergan (fan)

A lot of fans couldn't get over to Leigh

I was at the semi-final at Leigh and it was a mid-week game, but because I was working for myself then I was able to schedule my work to make sure that I was able to go to the game, I was winding down to retirement, so I wasn't taking on too much work. I remember that there weren't many Batley fans there, probably because it was a mid-week game and therefore a lot of fans couldn't get over to Leigh. That meant that there wasn't much of an atmosphere after the match because relatively few Batley supporters were there. The Leigh fans didn't like losing, especially as they had expected to beat us relatively easily, whereas it was the opposite that happened. Officials at Leigh had been talking about the final before the semi-final had even been played. I heard that they had been booking coaches to the Final, which was a bit disrespectful to Batley.

Anyway, it backfired on them. My daughter was at the game with me and after the game we went back to the Nash and we had a pretty good night even though there were quite a few people in the Nash who didn't realise that Batley had won a semi-final.

Ged Littlewood (fan)

Winding up Robbie Paul

I wasn't able to get to the semi-final against Leigh because it was on a Thursday evening (17th June) and I was working until 6:00pm, so I watched it on Sky round at my mate's place. I think that Batley's performance against Leigh was their best performance that season.

Leigh had a strong team and they battered us in the first part of the game but we stood firm and they didn't have any answers. I remember one particular incident during the match when one of the Leigh players broke through on the left side of the field and it looked as though he was certain to score but Jonny Campbell clattered him into touch. Leigh tried everything, but they just couldn't break us down. After that tackle by Jonny, they looked like a beaten side. Batley turned up the heat then, started scoring and Leigh didn't have any answers.

I remember that when the draw for the semi-finals took place on Radio Leeds and it came out as Leigh v Batley and Keighley v Widnes, Robbie Paul (Leigh player) said "That's the right draw, because Leigh v Widnes is the Final that everyone wants to see."

I think that the radio journalist (it might have been James Deighton) pointed out that the final could be Keighley v Batley, or some other combination that the fans of the participating teams would want to see.

Apparently during the semi-final, Danny Maun was winding Robbie Paul up throughout the match by referring to him as Henry

(Robbie's more famous brother) and saying stuff like "I thought you were a great player when you were at Bradford, Henry."

John Miller (Director, Batley RLFC)

Danny Maun didn't miss a tackle

I wasn't able to go to the semi-final at Leigh because it was a mid-week evening game and I was working, so I couldn't get over to Leigh. I watched it on TV at the Nash. I remember that Leigh had been the hot favourites amongst the press and the commentators, but in the end we won very comfortably.

I can remember that Danny Maun had a great defensive game. He didn't miss a tackle and he didn't give Leigh any room to move. That was true of the whole team. Batley's strong defence, throughout the team, wore Leigh down. By the end of the match Leigh were dejected and could not breach the Batley defence, so eventually Batley scored some tries and it was a very convincing victory.

Barry Dale (fan)

Have we really done this?

I never liked going to Leigh because I thought that the stewards were overzealous and that it wasn't a very welcoming place. I went on the Supporters' Club bus and I can remember Colin Bottomley flying a flag on the field before the game.

It was a fantastic victory and I can remember thinking have we really done this because Leigh had been strong favourites to win the cup. Then it was a question of dare to dream, and can we actually do it? Everybody was buzzing.

Janet Virr (fan)

The Leigh fans were shocked

I went to the semi-final against Leigh. It was on a Thursday night and what I remember is that even though we won convincingly in the end, the first half was very tight and there was hardly anything in it. I remember that just before half-time Lee Greenwood should have gone in at the corner, so that was a bit disappointing and you begin to think is that what it's going to be like, you know, near misses and missed chances, but then in the second half we did start to get on top and there's no doubt that we rattled Leigh. Gareth Moore put Danny Maun in and then we started to dominate. This was not something they were expecting.

They had a strong side, but our forwards had the measure of their pack. Paddy Hesketh , Byron Smith and Gallagher were very good. Paul Handforth was outstanding. He was guiding the team round the field, thinking about openings. Jonny Campbell had a tremendous game at full back. He put in some crucial tackles and it was that sort of thing which broke the back of the Leigh side. They couldn't get through and we stopped them getting into the game.

You have to remember that we were massive underdogs even though we'd beaten them the week before.

They'd put out a weakened team, but the signs were there that they might underestimate us. Robbie Paul had been going on about how the final would be between Leigh and Widnes, how that would be right. That's not showing enough respect to a team like Batley.

He played in the semi-final and I think that he had some sort of groin injury, because his thigh was heavily strapped up, so he probably wasn't 100 per cent fit. Maybe he thought that it wouldn't matter against Batley because Leigh weren't expecting Batley to do 'em.

Normally, Leigh supporters hadn't been all that friendly towards Batley supporters, but after this match instead of getting some abuse they were saying that the best side had won, which was good. I suppose it's hard to argue with a score like that (4-25).

Leigh certainly didn't think that they would only manage to get one try against Batley. I could see that some of the fans were shocked because it wasn't as though we'd sneaked a win; we'd beaten them convincingly.

Malcolm Westerby (fan)

We hammered them

I didn't go to the semi-final, but I watched it live at Birstall Nash. That was a fantastic performance because we didn't just win the match but we hammered them. I have a specific memory of a Jonny Campbell tackle on one of the Leigh players who was heading for what would have been a certain try. There is no doubt that this was a huge win for Batley because Leigh were very strong favourites to win the Cup.

John Atkins (fan)

A lesson in tight teamwork

I don't remember a great deal about the campaign, but I do remember that when we played at Leigh in the semi-final, they were already sorting the ticketing out for the final. They were assuming that they would beat us to get to the Final. There was an announcement before the game started that tickets for the final would be on sale after the match. Of course, some fans might have wanted to go to the final irrespective of who was in the final, but it seemed that they were being rather presumptuous in assuming that they would definitely beat us. As it happened, we gave them a lesson in the value of tight teamwork and determined effort because we won easily. In fact, it gave us a bit of a boost, because it made us more determined to win.

Kevin Nicholas (Chairman, Batley RLFC)

The press reports of Batley's semi-final win simply reinforce the testimony of both fans and players.

The Yorkshire Post, 18th June, 2010, noted that Batley "were in dreamland after holding Leigh Centurions for most of the opening period….in the end, winning in comfortable fashion." According to this newspaper "Batley hit a purple patch in the last ten minutes."

The Batley News, 24th June, 2010, offered a precise and succinct summary of Batley's unexpected victory: "The Bulldogs raised their game to new heights last Thursday and swept into the Northern Rail Cup Final with an outstanding performance at Leigh Sports Village ... Some of the Bulldogs tackling near their line was outstanding, with Jason Walton and Ash Lindsay setting a huge lead but the rest were quick to follow ... Campbell made a tremendous tackle to sweep Dave Alstead into touch near the line. It was virtually Leigh's last real threat as the Batley tackling intensified."

2.

PREPARATIONS FOR BLACKPOOL

BATLEY'S COACH, KARK HARRISON, was determined to keep the preparations for the Northern Rail Cup Final as low key as possible, though it was inevitable that some adjustments to the normal routine would have to be made.

We cut the shirts out of the cloth

We had a few weeks to prepare, and to order new kit for the match. Gareth Moore's father made the kit at Xblades.

I went to work on the Tuesday morning and Iro (Paul Harrison) said we have got a job on this morning. I said what's that apart from selling tickets for the big game and he said that we would have to go to Xblades to give them a hand as they were so busy. So, me and Iro ended up cutting the shirts out of the cloth for them to sew.

You couldn't make it up. We had a laugh about it.

Jonathan Hooley (kitman)

The Heavy Woollen Victories

An event at the Nash

After that win against Leigh it was very hectic because I was working during the day and then selling tickets in the evening because the easiest way for fans to get them was to come up to the club.

We had an event at the Nash on the Friday night, where the players paraded in front of the customers. They weren't there for very long, but Karl thought that it was important for the team to make an appearance there because quite a lot of fans were customers at the Nash.

John Miller (Director, Batley RLFC)

They were interested that we are brothers

It was a fantastic experience for me, particularly with me having played for the club for a long time and the family connection with Karl as the coach.

It was so special just getting to the final and, of course, in the build-up to the game there was such a lot of excitement amongst the fans and everybody at the club. It was really hectic selling tickets and getting transport organised for the day of the final. It was just something very special.

There were things happening that wouldn't have been happening normally at Batley. People wanted interviews with Karl and some of the players. I think that I was interviewed as well, even though things were pretty frantic. They were interested in the fact that me and Karl are brothers. It was different for the players as well because they wouldn't normally get that sort of attention.

'Calendar' wanted to interview some of the players for the TV. We didn't usually have a TV camera crew at the ground. Karl was keen to keep it as normal as possible. Obviously, the players were bound to get more nervous than normal because it was a special game.

Paul Harrison (Chief Executive, Batley RLFC)

I talked about my experience of playing in big games

We didn't do anything special with regard to our preparations for the final. In the week before, it was a fairly typical training week.

On the Tuesday, we put the previous game to bed, then there were talks with individuals and some analysis of videos. On the Thursday, more video work and a focus on how we wanted to play and then on the Friday, we had the team run.

On the day of the final we set off quite early on the coach and stopped at the 'Tickled Trout' near Preston for a coffee. Everybody was excited and we had a private room there. I did a team talk there and talked about my experience of playing in big games, because most of the team didn't have that sort of experience and these sorts of occasions can get to you.

I had that experience and that is what I talked about rather than tactics for the game itself because we'd already done that. I thought that the main thing was to try and put the players at ease and give them the benefit of my experience of handling big games.

I thought about my debut for Great Britain in 1990. This was the first time that I had played at representative level.

Andy Gregory, who's a few years older than me, came over to me and asked if I was nervous. I told him that I was and he said that when we walked out onto the pitch, I shouldn't look up to see the crowd or to try and spot family members or a girlfriend. He said that I should just keep my head down and then get on with the game.

When we were at the 'Tickled Trout', I spoke about this to the players and how it had helped me deal with the occasion. When the Batley team walked out onto the pitch at Blackpool, about 95% of the team did what Andy Gregory had advised me to do. They were totally focused and ready for the game.

Karl Harrison

That made sense to me

There weren't really any special preparations for the final. It was just more of the same. Karl had a few chats with us and he was trying to relax us and give us the benefit of his own playing experience because he had played at a high level. He gave us some advice about what to do when we came out of the tunnel onto the field.

He suggested that we just keep our heads down and keep focused on the pitch, not looking around to see who we could spot in the crowd, so that we could wave to them. He said that there would be plenty of time to do that at the end of the match. That made sense to me. It's the prima donnas who are likely to be doing that sort of thing and we didn't have anybody like that in the team. It was important to focus on what we were there for and that was to win the match.

Sean Hesketh

We had to match them in the forwards

In the week before the final we trained really well, but we didn't do anything special. Karl wanted us to be tough and difficult to beat. We knew that Widnes had some good players and that Thackeray would be one of their key men. Ainscough was at Widnes then and he was a good player, who came to Batley later. They had a big pack and, of course, they were desperate to get back into Super League, so we knew that we would have to match them in the forwards.

Danny Maun

Why change something which had been successful

We didn't really do anything special for the final. We just went about our jobs in the team in the same way as we had done before. We just did our standard training in the week before the final.

Karl Harrison's attitude was that there was no need to do anything different. Why change something which had been successful. He'd brought the team together and he'd kept Batley up the previous season. If you start changing things for one game, then that's when it can go wrong. The way we were playing was working and that's what was important. I think that the general attitude was that we were not going to let this opportunity slip because we had all worked so hard to get there. Most of us were local players, so we were a close-knit group. Ash Lindsay used to inspire others because even when he was out on his feet, he would find that little bit extra to carry on and that would lift other players. The key thing was that all the players bought into that mentality. It's no good having just two thirds of the team turning up; you need the whole lot pulling together. That's how we had avoided relegation in 2009.

Paul Handforth

There were people in Asda wishing me good luck

We didn't really do anything different from what we normally did. Karl Harrison used to do a lot of full contact stuff unlike what other coaches did, and we did that on Tuesday. The only different thing that I can remember is that we got brand new shirts for the final and there was a bit of a panic as to whether they would be done in time. The buzz around the club was amazing. For a change, the media were interested in us and Paul and Karl Harrison were talking to the media and we just got on with our usual training.

Widnes were expected to win the final. The press were saying that it was great that Batley had got to the final. That was an achievement, but they didn't expect us to win it. I don't know what odds the bookies were giving, but I bet there were some good ones, so I hope some fans had a good win out of it. I got texts from people I'd not heard from, wishing me good luck. There were people in Asda wishing me good luck for Sunday. We weren't superstars, but there were still people waving to us and we were in the local press.

Kris Lythe

Karl gave us the freedom to play

I don't remember any special preparations for the final. We didn't stay overnight in Blackpool. We just got on the coach on the day. There was quite a gap between the semi-final and the final, so we had to focus on the games that had to be played during that time. By the time of the final we didn't have a particular game plan. Karl gave us the freedom to play how we needed to play and we had the players to do that. We could keep it tight if that was needed and the forwards could drive us up-field and then we could move the ball wide. We knew what we were doing, everyone was in tune with that.

Obviously, there was excitement in the team because most players had not been in this sort of final and probably thought this would be their one chance, but apart from that it was just the normal script.

Lee Greenwood

I was desperate to be on the field from the start

There was more media interest in Batley than normal; journalists from newspapers wanting to talk to people at the club and Look North came to do some interviews. Karl didn't do anything special. He wanted the build-up to be as relaxed and normal as possible.

We had a fairly small squad, so the emphasis was on keeping everybody fit. It was the normal weekly training and on Thursday evening Karl named the squad. I was desperate to be on the field from the start rather than coming off the bench, which was a possibility. It had been my best season because I'd been mainly free from injury, so I was delighted when I was selected at centre.

Me and Lee Greenwood were on the right side, but the general plan was to go down more on their right hand side to try and put pressure on their half-back, Thackeray, who was one of their playmakers. The idea was to tire him out by making him have to do plenty of tackling.

Mark Toohey

He tried to take the pressure off us

Karl was a very good coach and he was meticulous in his preparation, but he didn't go out of his way to do things differently in the build-up to the final. We did the same training and went through the same routines. Karl knew that it was a really big game for the players, so there were a few team talks, but he wanted us to approach it as far as we could like any other game. He tried to take the pressure off us as much as he could. I mean there was a lot more activity around the club than usual. The local press and media were interested far more than they would normally have been, but Karl didn't want us to be distracted by all that. Playing in the final was a big deal for the team because we had the chance to do something that the club had not been able to do for a long time. I had a bit more experience than some of the players because I'd been at Hull KR and Toulouse and I'd played in a couple of semi-finals.

There was a massive buzz within the club and everybody was looking forward to the match, so it was a case of remaining as calm as possible and not getting over-excited. It was special for me because I'm from Batley. We were all ready to go on the day and we believed that we could beat them, even though we knew that it wouldn't be easy. Experienced players like Paul Handforth and Karl had cool heads. Paul was very professional on the field and they were both building us up for the game, encouraging us to just play our game. They had a calming effect on the team.

Tommy Gallagher

The training was always physical

We didn't do anything special in the week before the final. Karl was just trying to keep us relaxed because he knew how big a game it was for the team and the club. He trained us hard but you could always have a good laugh with Karl and that's what we needed. We were a bit nervous, but the training was always physical. It was full on tackling, and Karl didn't shy away from that. He wanted his players properly prepared, so even before a big game it was full contact. Karl knew that players saw it as a chance to be selected. They could show him what they were made of.

There was a lot more press and media interest than there would normally have been at Batley, not so much for me but for the more experienced players. The media were interested in Tiger Handforth as he was one of the key players. I was trying to ignore the extra attention the club was getting because I wanted to focus on the game.

John Gallagher

No short cuts in training

We all believed in each other and there was a real buzz around the team in the week before the final. There wasn't really any special preparation in training for the final. It was just more of the same.

Karl was a believer in full contact training; no short cuts. After the semi-final, I felt as though I'd been hit by a car, but you just had to go straight back into training. We'd given 110 per cent in that game and luckily I'd not suffered any injury. We had a decent size squad, so that helped Karl because he could see who was ready and whether anyone was carrying an injury. Everybody was wondering whether they would be picked for the final.

There were some players who'd had good games in earlier rounds who didn't play in the semi, but some people had to be left out. Mark Barlow had had some good games, but he wasn't picked. The main thing was that everybody had contributed for us to get to the final.

Ash Lindsay

I booked Monday off as well

I wasn't at the semi-final because I was working, so as soon as I found out that Batley had beaten Leigh I immediately booked that weekend off and the Monday as well because I knew that whatever happened, I wouldn't want to have to go in to work on the Monday.

One of my mates from work came to the final with me. I had got my ticket at Batley's ground and you could book a seat on the coach over the phone or pay on the day, when you got on the coach at the Frontier. I think that it cost £10 or £15 for the coach. I think I've still got a ticket stub from the coach, because I keep stuff like that.

Richard Drake (fan)

Good luck from New Zealand

I would like to extend my best wishes to the Bulldogs this coming Sunday in their quest to win the Northern Rail Cup in Blackpool. I would like to think that the people of Batley will get behind them and give them their full support. They are creating a lot of publicity for the town and deserve all the encouragement they can get.

Frank Riley
Glendene, Auckland, New Zealand

The above letter which appeared in the Batley News, *15th July, 2010, and which was presumably sent to the newspaper by a former citizen of Batley, is reminiscent of a letter that was printed in the* Batley News and Birstall Advertiser, *25th May, 1885, in which a Mr C. Wilson of Manayunk, USA, described how a group of former Batley citizens celebrated Batley's 1885 victory in the Yorkshire Challenge Cup final.*

What odds on a Batley victory?

The fact that Widnes were favourites to beat Batley in the Northern Rail Cup final should come as no great surprise, most especially as they had been in Super League as recently as 2005.

However, there was, and still is, a degree of resentment amongst Batley fans that their team was not given the respect it deserved in the run-up to the final. Of course, it may also be the case that the fans' perception of how Batley was treated by the press and pundits was filtered through the prism of what they expected to hear based on past experience. In the event, those fans who liked to have a bet were able to benefit from the generous odds that were being offered on the chances of Batley winning the trophy.

When Batley won, I was quids in

I wasn't able to go to the semi-final against Leigh, so I watched it on TV. My son went. When I found out that Batley had beaten Leigh, I put £20 on Batley at 22/1 to win the Northern Rail Cup. It was crackers. Batley won, I was quids in. The bookies were still offering 7/1 close to the date of the match, so my mates each put ten quid on Batley. I mean, offering 22/1 in a 'two horse race'; that must have been someone who didn't know what they were doing.

John McVeigh (fan)

It was certainly worth a bet

Some fans did pretty well by putting a bet on Batley to win because you were able to get quite long odds on a Batley win and some betting companies were offering 20 or 30 points start. That was certainly worth a bet because we didn't think that we would lose by 30 points. I mean, we had beaten Leigh pretty easily in the semi-final and they had not expected that.

Richard Drake (fan)

Demeaning comments

Some ocomments being made about the players by pundits and journalists were demeaning. They were saying that the Batley players were rat catchers and road sweepers and things like that. Some were not saying anything about their ability as rugby players.

Grahame Hobson (fan)

Batley just there to make up the numbers

Even though we had beaten Leigh, the pundits didn't give us much chance. As far as they were concerned, Batley was just there to make up the numbers. We had drawn with Widnes up at the Mount earlier in the season and then we had beaten them at Widnes. It was as if the pundits and commentators hadn't been taking any notice of what had happened during the season.

Barry Lee (fan)

The same old story

The press hadn't given us much chance of beating Leigh and they didn't give us much chance of winning the cup against Widnes, even though we had beaten Leigh and we had drawn with Widnes at home in February. It's a bit like the reports this weekend which described Batley's win at Featherstone as a surprising or unexpected victory. We had already drawn with Featherstone at home and then beaten them at Featherstone, so I don't see why it was unexpected. I think that sort of reporting is disrespectful to Batley and doesn't give the club the credit it deserves. It was like that in 2010. The press were more or less saying that Batley were there in the Final just to make up the numbers.

Billy Lonergan (fan)

Maybe some people hadn't noticed

I can recall that there was plenty of speculation that Widnes would walk the final. There is no doubt that Batley were the underdogs, but Karl Harrison had turned the team's fortunes around even though he had only been at Batley for eighteen months.

Maybe some people hadn't noticed, but Batley hadn't just beaten Leigh, they had destroyed them even though Leigh had been strong favourites to win the Northern Rail Cup in 2010. Widnes looked like the stronger team on paper, but the gap between Batley and Widnes was nowhere near as big as some of the pundits were suggesting.
Robert Hicks (referee)

It's disrespectful

I remember that the media speculation was focused on how a team like Batley had managed to get to this stage. To some extent there is still the same attitude at some of the bigger clubs in the Championship when we beat them. They say we shouldn't be beaten by teams like Batley. It's a bit disrespectful.

Janet Virr (fan)

Fans probably didn't expect to win

As I remember, it was the usual stuff in the press and on the radio about Batley being the underdogs and Widnes the strong favourites. I think it was probably only the members of the team who thought that they were going to win. The fans were looking forward to having a weekend in Blackpool and probably didn't expect to win. They were going to have a good time, whatever the result. They were going more in hope than in expectation of a win, even though Batley had beaten some good teams to get there.

Craig Lingard (ex-player, coach and fan)

The Spenborough Guardian *16th July, 2010, adopted an admirably objective approach to the upcoming Northern Rail Cup Final by focusing on statistics.*

It noted that Batley were the competition's top scorers with 261 points scored and 90 conceded, their average winning score being 43-15. Widnes, whose average winning score was 35-16, had scored 212 points and conceded 98, whilst with regard to the last ten matches between the clubs, Widnes held the advantage with six wins to Batley's three with one match drawn. The newspaper's conclusion was that the statistics pointed to a thriller!

3.

I DO LIKE TO BE BESIDE THE SEASIDE

SOME BATLEY FANS travelled to Blackpool on Sunday 19th July, 2010, the day of the Northern Rail Cup Final, whilst others arrived the day before in order to make the most of a weekend at the seaside.

My friend Heinz came over from Switzerland

I supplied the red and white flags that fans had on the day of the match. I didn't get them to make a profit, it was just a gesture to support the club. If possible, I just wanted to cover my costs.

My friend Heinz came over from Switzerland and a few of the lads from Marske went down to Blackpool. A few of them hadn't seen a rugby league match before, but they were attracted by the idea of a Saturday night in Blackpool. My friend Richard had a Mercedes bus to take his family to games and I begged a lift from him, because I was going to be interviewed on a radio broadcast on Radio Leeds because the story of my friend Heinz coming over from Switzerland had sparked some interest. We ran out of petrol about five miles

109

from where I was headed. Anyway, we did get interviewed by Radio Leeds on the Sunday morning, and they spoke to Heinz about why he had come over from Switzerland.

Walking round Blackpool on the Sunday morning, we didn't see many Batley supporters. I think that most of them went directly to the ground. There were plenty of Widnes supporters out and about. There was a lot of good-natured banter and when we were in the Galleon Bar the night before, it was crazy. You know, we were giving the Widnes fans some stick, but in a nice way. There was a lot of back and forth.

We stayed in a hotel/B&B in Blackpool. It was a dump. I remember that the landlady was called Julie and she was a right 'un. I had booked several people into the place for a couple of nights and when I arrived, the first thing that she said was "Have you got the money?" No words of welcome, or anything like that. I think it was called the Beachfield Hotel, and calling it a hotel was a very generous description. One of my mates from Whitby just stayed one night and then he went on to Trip Advisor and absolutely slated the place. The only thing is, he posted the comments in my name.

Of course, the landlady saw it and I was staying in the place for two nights, so she had a right go at me. My mate hadn't said anything that was inaccurate, but it was too bad he'd done it in my name when I was still there. In fact, the only reason I had booked it was because there were a lot of positive reviews on Trip Advisor. She must have put them on herself. Heinz had brought a cowbell from Switzerland and left it in the hotel, so another lad had to go back and get it for him on the night of the game. He got some stick from the landlady.

We stayed up drinking till three o' clock in the morning on the first night and when I got up for breakfast, one of my mates, a Scottish bloke, was still drinking at the bar. He hadn't bothered to go to bed. His eyes were out on stalks during the game.

On the Sunday morning, being a good Roman Catholic, I went to mass, but the church I walked to didn't have a mass on that Sunday morning. Anyway, a priest arrived in his car and he took me to another church where he was doing the mass. I thought that we needed all the help we could get.

Outside the Blackpool ground there was a sort of working men's club. I think it was the Tangerine Club. Anyway, there were people in there playing bingo, or trying to because there were twenty Batley lads singing at the top of their voices. They threw us out, which was fair enough.

John McVeigh (fan)

He came over from Colombia

Bruce Thewlis, who was at Batley Boys' High School, came over from Colombia for the match. He still lives there. He has a very successful business growing flowers in Colombia.

Whenever he came back to Batley to visit family, he always came the Mount to watch a game. He used to be in the Taverners and when he bought some drinks he handed over a fifty pound note for each round because he couldn't be bothered to sort out the change from the previous round (classic 'boozer's pocket'.)

I remember that there was torrential rain on the way to Blackpool, all the way on the M55. There were huge puddles.

Grahame Hobson (fan)

Fish 'n chips

I went to the match with Stuart, my daughter and both grandsons. We had a great day, arriving in the morning and having fish 'n chips at a restaurant. None of our group thought that we were going to win. We were just going for a good day out.

John Cresswell (fan)

No trains

It was the Northern Rail Cup Final, but ironically Northern Rail cancelled the trains to Blackpool, so fans had to go there in coaches or private cars.

Grahame Hobson (fan)

The Heavy Woollen Victories

Didn't expect to win

We went by car and probably would have done even if the trains had been running. I didn't expect to see Batley win because we hadn't won anything significant since 1924. We just went with the intention of having a good day out and we were not disappointed.

David Hopkin (fan)

We were mingling with Batley and Widnes fans

We met up at the Frontier early morning. That's where the coaches were setting off from because there was plenty of space for them to park and then they could head off to the motorway because the Frontier was on a main road. They opened the bar early at the Frontier so that we could get a drink and we were all wearing Batley polo shirts we'd got from Ravensport. I think that we set off about 9:00am, so we arrived in Blackpool between 11:00am and 12:00. As far as I can remember, the coaches were full. There might have been the odd spare seat, probably because someone had been out boozing the night before and they had missed the coach because they hadn't got up in time.

When we got to Blackpool, we all met up and went to various bars because the match didn't start until 4:00pm. We were mingling with Batley and Widnes fans and it was all good humoured. You know, there was lots of banter between the Batley and Widnes fans and some serious discussion about rugby league as well. I mean, Batley fans were not expecting to win. They wanted to see a good game but Widnes were favourites to win and their fans expected them to win.

We got to the ground about half an hour before the kick-off after we had been all round the town; you know into all the bars. When we got into the ground we went and got some drinks and we were all sitting together behind the sticks at one end.

As I said, we didn't want to get hammered by Widnes but most of us went to Blackpool to watch Batley play in an important Final and have a good day out. Widnes, I think, had just got their new stadium and they had some fairly big-name players. It was only five years since they had been in Super League.

Richard Drake (fan)

We were wearing bespoke shirts

I went on a coach organised by the Supporters' Club. It left from the ground, but most of the coaches left from the Frontier and I'm not sure who organised that because I think that there were about 12 coaches went from there. We'd got our tickets up at the ground.

We got there pretty early and we walked round Blackpool for an hour or so before we went to the ground. We were wearing bespoke shirts because my mate, who worked at a printing firm, had made three shirts specially for the final. They were shirts that were specially adapted for the final. Originally, they had been shirts sponsored by Kozee Sleep, but my mate had overprinted Gallant Youths on the Kozee Sleep logo, which was just as well because I wouldn't have worn that shirt again with the Kozee Sleep logo on it because the owner had been sent to jail for his involvement in trafficking people. So, we were wearing unique shirts.

Barry Lee (fan)

He got changed into a green fluorescent mankini

I was over the moon that we'd go to the final, but I didn't expect that we would win. I mean Widnes had a quality side, even their substitutes. It looked as though they had too much strength in depth for us.

I went on a coach from the White Hart, just up the road from Fox's Biscuits, on the opposite side of the road. In fact, there were buses going from various places I think that it was probably Jimmy Hooley who organised the coaches from the White Hart. There were two or three that went on the day. I'm not sure how I found out about the coach, whether it was posted in the pub, or whether it was advertised in the local paper. It was a great atmosphere. I wore the red and white strip that Batley were playing in at the time.

We went there and came back on the match day and we went to the Frontier when we got back to Batley. I think that we arrived in Blackpool at about lunchtime and we had a few pints before going to the ground. There were quite a lot of Batley fans in Blackpool, but there were more Widnes fans. You could see that as you walked round Blackpool, but that was not surprising because Widnes were a bigger club with more supporters and it's a bit closer to Blackpool.

One pub we were in, a bloke who had played for Batley Boys came in and went into the toilets where he got changed into a green fluorescent mankini. He came out of the toilets into the bar with his hands in the air. It still tickles me to think about it. All the Widnes fans who were in the pub cheered. He walked from the pub to the ground and he was cheered all the way en route by both sets of fans. What a laugh! I'm not sure whether he was allowed into the ground wearing the mankini. It might have been that one of his mates brought his clothes up to the ground and he got changed before he went in.

John McGowan (fan and ex-Batley player)

They were not going to let me in

It was my friend's unofficial stag do and I took the mankini with me on the proviso that he'd be wearing it. He said no, but then I thought that it would be a brilliant idea for me to wear it, just for effect.

I put it on in a pub near to where the coach had dropped us off and I got a few laughs. I carried on wearing it in the pub, but then as it was getting near kick-off time I was wondering whether I should get changed. Then I thought "No, I'm going to the ground wearing it." I got a barrel of laughs on the way there. I'd done similar things before, so people who knew me were not surprised and photos were taken. I left my rugby socks on, which looked a bit strange with the mankini

When I got to the ground they were not going to let me in, so I was panicking. I had to prove that I wasn't drunk. That was the reason why they were not letting me in because they thought that I was drunk. I mean, I was a bit merry but that was as much from the excitement of the day as anything else. Batley were in a final and had the chance of winning some silverware and that wasn't something I'd experienced before. The closest had been when we played Doncaster for a place in the top division.

I was begging them to let me in and saying I'm sober and I can walk straight. Eventually they said that I didn't sound drunk, so if I put my clothes back on, they would let me in. One of the mum's from Batley Boys had brought my clothes and I was able to get dressed. They confiscated the mankini. They let me in, but they told me that the camera would be on me and if I took my clothes off I would be escorted out of the ground. This panicked me a bit because I certainly didn't want to be thrown out. I think that if it had been a football match, they wouldn't have let me in.

Darren Rhodes (fan)

We had a good walk around Blackpool

I went over to Blackpool by car and my son-in-law drove. I'd got the tickets up at the ground to make sure that we were with the Batley fans. We just went to Blackpool for the day. We didn't stay over, even though it was a four o'clock kick-off.

It was July, so it was light until late on and we'd get back before it was dark. We made sure that we got to Blackpool in good time and we went to a pub, The Manchester, near the pleasure beach, that I was familiar with from day trips. It was a pub where there were sometimes more bouncers than customers. The sort of place where your feet were sticking to the floor.

We got there at opening time and we didn't stay that long because they were still clearing up from the previous night; there were still some bottles on the bar. Then we had a good walk round Blackpool because it was a nice day. It was July and it was busy with day trippers and holidaymakers. We saw fans from different clubs, not just Batley and Widnes fans but from clubs like Wigan and other Lancashire clubs. It was one of the best rugby league days that I can remember. We went to a café in Blackpool and had some fish and chips and then we got to the ground at about 3:30pm and it was already quite full. We were just about behind the posts with a lot of other Batley fans, though Batley fans were outnumbered in the ground by Widnes fans and Widnes were the red-hot favourites.

There was a bit of a buzz amongst the Batley fans even though they didn't expect to win. A lot of Batley fans were there to enjoy a good day out because it was the first time Batley had been in a major final for a lot of years.

Allan Waite (fan of Bradford Bulls)

I had to wear a shirt and a club tie

After the semi-final, Paul (Harrison) told me that there was room for me on the Directors' bus and I thought "that'll be better than driving." We have a lot of connections with the club because of Paul who's married to our eldest daughter, Rebecca. When Paul was playing at Hull we supported him there and then when he moved to play for Batley, we switched allegiance.

I came back from Rugby for the weekend and Paul told me that I would have to wear a shirt and a club tie as I was going with the Directors. This was something that I wouldn't normally do if I was going to a match. I used to wear a shirt and tie during the week when I was working and at the weekends I would wear a casual shirt, or a replica shirt if I was going to a game. Anyway, I thought "sacrifices have to be made."

Paul told us to come to Batley's ground for bacon sandwiches before we set off on the coach, which seemed like a good idea. My wife, Gwynneth, was on the coach as well. When we arrived in Blackpool, the coach took us directly to the ground, we went upstairs into the Directors' suite and all the tables and chairs were set out for dining. We had a meal and then we went to our seats in the stadium.

Stuart Merton (fan)

Heavy Woollen solidarity

I got my ticket from the club and I went on the Supporters' Club coach, because at the time I was the Treasurer of the Supporters'

Club. The coach picked us up at Aldi. Normally there would have been spare seats on the Supporters' Club coach but this time it was chock-a-block, absolutely packed. Sometimes it had been a struggle to get enough on the coach to make it viable, but not this time. There were other coaches as well down by Aldi, but I'm not sure whether they were organised by the Supporters' Club or whether they were independents.

We got to Blackpool reasonably early because we wanted to have time to have a look around and breathe in some of the sea air. It was July and it was gorgeous weather. I'm not sure whether we expected Batley to win, but we knew they were a very competent side, so we expected that they would give a good showing. The team had confidence in Karl. He's a man of few words, who only talks when necessary and only says what needs to be said.

I was on the coach with two mates who were Huddersfield Town supporters and who had never been to watch Batley away from home, though they had been to some games at The Mount. We got bacon sarnies for breakfast. The coach parked up by the stadium and we had a walk on the sea front to take in the sea air. There were lots of rugby league fans walking about: Batley fans, Widnes fans and supporters from other rugby league clubs.

We went to the Manchester pub and had a couple of pints and then we went to a Wetherspoons by the Tower and then the Albert and Lion. There were a lot of Batley and Dewsbury fans at the Wetherspoons because it was cheap beer. It's a big pub and it was mainly filled with Batley supporters. The Dewsbury fans were wearing T-shirts which said " A Dog for today but a Ram forever," which was a nice gesture. Heavy Woollen solidarity I suppose.

There were quite a few people in Wetherspoons who I knew. There were some who had played for Dewsbury Celtic. It was a great atmosphere because the fans were just there to enjoy themselves. We had some fish 'n chips and then we headed through the backstreets to the ground because we'd been told that it was quicker than walking back on the sea front; it wasn't. It was a long drag with nothing interesting to see. We saw Mick Bedford and his mate coming out of a slop house where they'd had something to eat and we went with them to the Albert and Lion for a couple of pints. Outside the pub we met Pamela and Steve Grinhaff and Pamela's identical twin, Patricia.

I hadn't been to Blackpool for about twenty years and it had completely changed in that time. We used to go for weekends or to see a show when my son was young. I think that we got into the ground at about 2:30pm. We weren't directly behind the posts because I'm not so keen on that. You get fans shouting offside and forward pass when the play is at the other end and that's just stupid.

Billy Lonergan (fan)

The players were serious

On match day, we set off for Blackpool and can remember stopping off for a coffee at the white hotel near to Blackpool. Kevin gave a speech on what it meant to him and the club to win a trophy.

The players were serious. The look on their faces showed that they meant business. We got to the stadium and we were in the home dressing room. I saw the guy from Sky and told him again that we were going to win. He just laughed and said that the beers were on him if we won.

Jonathan Hooley (kitman)

We wrote in the sand

I got my ticket for the final up at the ground and the club organised coaches to go to the match. The coaches set off from the Frontier because there was plenty of space down there for them to park. I saw some people getting on the coaches who I hadn't seen for years. This is the problem with the gates at Batley. Where are all those people for ordinary league matches?

I made a banner and I've still got it. In fact, I took it along for the Million Pound Game on Sunday. I said back in 2010 that I would save it for the next big final. I adapted it from a flag that the Sun newspaper gave away. It was for some sort of jubilee celebration. When we gathered in the Market Place in Batley the following week to celebrate the cup win, I had the flag with me and it appeared on TV because the cameras were there for the local news. I had it with me on Sunday and Premier Sport filmed us with the banner. My two daughters were there with me.

When we arrived in Blackpool before the Northern Rail Final, we went onto the beach. It was throwing it down, but we used a stick to write in the sand "Batley, Northern Rail Cup Winners." We had a walk round Blackpool before the match and we were mingling with all the fans, including the Widnes fans. They were saying that they were going to win easily. The press didn't give us much of a chance of winning, just like they'd been when we played Leigh in the semi-final. I remember that Karl Harrison did a radio interview before the game and he was asked to predict what the score might be and he said something like "I'm just a lad from Drighlington. I can't speak posh."

Ged Littlewood (fan)

We went in a limo

For the final in Blackpool, my mate, John Atkins, arranged to hire a limo. He always said that if Batley got to a major final, he would go there in a limo. There were several of us in the limo, not just me and John. There was my son, my grandson, Terry Midgely, Steve Jordan and David Harrison and his dad. The limo driver told us not to be late getting back to the car after the game had finished, but we'll come to that later.

Steve Pickard (fan)

As it was the first time since I'd begun watching Batley many years before that Batley had reached a major final, I decided that I would splash out on a limousine to take us to the match at Blackpool. As it happened, I came across a bloke, when I was having a drink in the Black Bull on a Sunday lunchtime, who had a limo service. In fact, he had been one of the groomsmen at my wedding. He was called Brendan Hough and he had been to St Mary's. Anyway, we sorted it out and I think that it was a nine-seater. There's a photo of us outside the old Princess Cinema in Birstall. Brendan was the driver and he was very relaxed, even when we were waiting for one person after the presentation had been made.

We set off round about lunchtime because it was a four o'clock kick-off and I had to open the shop in the morning for the Sunday newspapers etc. When we got to Blackpool we had a pint and then made sure that we got into the stadium early. I have a photo taken inside the pub we were in and the bloke in the green mankini is in the background.

John Atkins (fan)

Just pleased that we were in a final

I drove over to Lancashire for the Final with my wife, my brother-in-law and his wife.

We stayed overnight in Liverpool on the Saturday night and then we drove up to Blackpool the following day. I didn't want to stay in Blackpool because I thought that it was a bit of a dump and Liverpool was more interesting. We stayed in a Toby Carvery where they had some rooms.

When we got to Blackpool, we parked in that big car park near the railway station and then we went to a pub near the ground. There were some Batley fans in there but there were a lot more Widnes fans there. It was all good humoured, but the Widnes fans were full of confidence. They were certainly expecting to win, whereas I was just very pleased that we had got to the final and I didn't really expect us to win.

The press didn't either. Widnes were the strong favourites and we were there to make up the numbers.

On paper, they had a stronger team and I think they had been playing well. Widnes were a better-known team as well, because they had been in Super League and it wasn't all that long ago that they had been winning trophies, so I suppose it was not surprising that they were the strong favourites.

Barry Dale (fan)

There was no seat number 25

We went on a coach organised by the Half-Way House in Heckmondwike, because there were a lot of different places that were running coaches to the match and that one was convenient for us. There weren't a lot of people that we knew on the coach because there were people who were not regular supporters but were going to the match because it was a final.

When we got to the ground at Blackpool, I can remember that my ticket, which I'd bought at the club, was number 25, but the block of seats that it was in only went up to 24. I was looking for my seat and I had visions of not being able to be behind the posts, which is where I like to be. Fortunately, there were spare seats, so it didn't matter.

Janet Virr (fan)

Wheelchair ruse

I know of two lads who blagged their way in by one pushing the other in a wheelchair ... first Batley try and the lad sat in the wheelchair jumped up ... bundled out.

Michael Holmes (fan)

Tagged

I went on a roller coaster had fish and chips and then had to go straight home cos my tag wouldn't let me out after 5:00pm

Ben Thirkill (fan)

The fans were not segregated

I drove over to Blackpool with my best mate and we had booked a hotel for the Sunday night so that we didn't have to drive back and could have a few drinks before and after the game. I can't actually remember how we got the tickets for the game. Before the match there were a lot of fans in the pubs and the bars in Blackpool; Batley fans, Widnes fans and fans from other clubs. It was a good atmosphere and the fans were not segregated like they are when there is a major soccer match. There were more Widnes fans than Batley fans, but that was expected. There were more Batley fans than at a normal game, the fair-weather supporters, but I did recognise some faces from when I had been playing. Some Batley supporters only turn out for the big games.

Craig Lingard (fan and ex-player)

'Stevo' was staying in our hotel

We got our tickets from the club and four of us went over to Blackpool by car on the Saturday, the day before the game and we stayed in a hotel called the Chequers Plaza, at the north end of Blackpool. It turned out that Stevo was staying in this hotel as well and when I saw him in the bar, I bought him a drink, but I didn't get one back, which fit with what I'd heard about him that he's pretty tight with his money!

We went over the day before the game because we wanted to make a weekend of it because Batley had been in a final like this for a long time. I'd never seen them play in anything like this, so it was a big occasion for us. On the way over to Blackpool we even saw some Dewsbury supporters' cars which had signs in saying 'Dogs for the day, but Rams for life', which was a nice gesture from their fans. They were obviously supporting their rivals against a bigger Lancashire club. We went for a few beers on the Saturday night. We went to a working men's club and then we went back to the hotel. I went to bed reasonably early, but the others stayed up drinking in the hotel bar. I wanted to be fit and lively for the following day!

On the Sunday we went for a few drinks before the game and we went to a pub called the Lifeboat, but we also went to one nearer the ground because my mate wanted to go there for the karaoke. I can't remember the name of the pub. It was a bit of a dump, but it had a good pint of Tetley's which made up for it not being that great a pub. We'd seen a few Widnes supporters in Blackpool the night before and then on the Sunday, but there were plenty of Batley supporters around as well. It was a very good atmosphere; a lot of banter, but no nastiness. You could tell that Widnes fans expected to win. Maybe they thought that it was a bit of a fluke that we had beaten Leigh in the semi-final, but they seemed confident that they were going to win.

Mick Bedford (fan)

Wiltshire Bulldogs

Before the match I went for a walk to the North Pier and all I saw was Batley people. They simply took over Blackpool for the day. I saw some people I recognised from years ago, who live away, and they had on jumpers which said 'Wiltshire Bulldogs' that they had sewn on them.

Malcolm Haig (fan) –
from a story in **The Dewsbury Reporter**, *23rd July, 2010*

It is interesting to note Malcolm's perception that Batley fans took over Blackpool for the day given that there were certainly more Widnes fans in Blackpool for the Northern Rail Cup Final. It may be that as it was Batley's first chance of a trophy for many years, Batley fans made their presence felt more forcefully than did the Widnes supporters who had tasted success more recently.

Thank God we'll be setting off soon

I organised the buses, which departed from the Frontier and helped them out on the Sunday morning.

I made sure that I got there early and I was the first one in the Frontier, so I was able to marshal people as they arrived.

The players' families started to arrive and the wife of one of the players said to me 'thank God we'll be setting off fairly soon because he's been awake since 4:00am and he's been doing my head in, keeping me awake!'

John Miller (Director, Batley RLFC)

Good luck messages from ex-players

I travelled to Blackpool with the players and their wives/girlfriends. My son Joe was sitting further back in the coach. It was a great experience for him. I asked one of the wives /girlfriends if she wanted a cup of tea and she told me to get her bag down from the rack because she preferred to have some alcohol that she'd obviously got in her bag. When we got to Blackpool, me and Joe went for a walk and met up in a pub with my sister Sheila and her husband. The pub was absolutely rammed with Widnes supporters, so we stood out a mile as we were wearing Batley shirts. Of course, we received some good-natured stick from the Widnes fans. In other bars there were lots of Batley fans. It just so happened that the one in which we met Sheila was full of Widnes fans.

While we had been on the bus, travelling to Blackpool, I received a lot of good luck messages by text from ex-players. One of them cycled to Blackpool, but went back on the train. It felt as though it was a really special day. I think that the coach I was on arrived in Blackpool between 1:30 and 2:00pm. I'd arrived at the Frontier between 8:00 and 9:00am, but our coach was the last one to set off. The players were quite nervy when they got to Blackpool because there were still a couple of hours remaining before the kick-off.

John Miller (Director, Batley RLFC)

We met the Widnes directors before the game

On match day, I remember that we stopped off at the 'Tickled Trout', near Preston, on the way to Blackpool. We could have gone straight to Blackpool without stopping, but we decided that it would be useful to have a break for about an hour before we got to Blackpool. I had been past the place a few times when I had had to go to Preston prison and I thought it looked ok.

They let us have a room to ourselves and we had a little bit to eat, it wouldn't have been much. We had a short team meeting, but Karl didn't say very much and I don't think that I said anything at all. Sometimes I said a few words before a game, but on this occasion

I'm pretty sure I didn't speak and there weren't any questions from the team. They knew how much they were going to be paid and they knew it was less than Widnes were getting. I think that the WAGs went on a separate coach and it was just the players, backroom staff and the directors on our coach.

We met the Widnes directors before the match. I knew the Widnes chairman because I had met him previously at some RFL function and I got on with him. He was a decent bloke. He was a millionaire and he hadn't been at the club very long but he had put a fair bit of money into the club. He wasn't brash. He was quite a modest bloke (Steve O'Connor) and I think he had installed a woman who worked for him as the Chief Executive. They were both very nice people, very friendly. We had a chat before the game.

Kevin Nicholas (Chairman, Batley RLFC)

A calm atmosphere on the bus

The whole day seemed to fly by, but whilst we were waiting in the changing rooms for the start of the game, that seemed to take ages. On the bus over to Blackpool it was a calm atmosphere. We thought that we could win it and we were all ready for the game.

It was amazing going out onto the field because the Batley fans, even though there were more Widnes fans there, seemed to fill the ground. It was unreal, a fantastic atmosphere with all those Batley shirts in the crowd.

Tommy Gallagher

'Tiger' saw how nervous I was

It was quieter than usual going over on the coach, whereas we'd usually be having a laugh and some people would be playing cards. Normally, in the changing room before a match I would be laughing and joking, but this time I was the first to get changed and I just sat there, silent. 'Tiger' saw how nervous I was and he came over and spoke to me. He'd seen that I wasn't behaving the way I normally did and that helped me.

The Heavy Woollen Victories

When we went out onto the field I got a massive adrenalin rush and then it really came home to me how big an occasion it was. It was the first time I'd played in a game of such magnitude. I thought that there would just be loads of Widnes fans, but seeing all those Batley fans behind the sticks was a massive lift. I could see faces I recognised who'd been at all the Batley games.

John Gallagher

No overnight stay

We hadn't stayed overnight for any other games and we didn't for the final and that was part of not doing anything different from what we normally did. We met up at the club and I think that we might have had a bit of breakfast before we set off for Blackpool. There was a bit of nervousness in the dressing room and we knew that Widnes were massive favourites, but we got off to a good start with a couple of tries and that settled a few nerves.

Paul Handforth

We didn't have an overnight stay; we just went over to Blackpool on the day of the game. My family were there, my wife and two kids and there were some work colleagues as well. When we were in the dressing room we were trying to think of the match as just another game, but there were a lot more nerves than usual.

Mark Toohey

4.

NORTHERN RAIL CUP
FINAL – 18th JULY 2010

Widnes started to panic a bit

We started well and got a couple of early tries, but we always knew that if we got into the lead, Widnes would come back at us. I remember the atmosphere when we walked out onto the pitch for the warm-up. It was brilliant. I'd never seen so many Batley fans. That gave us a big lift and I don't know if all fans realise how important that is. It gives you that extra bit to not miss a tackle or to run that bit harder. It was great.

Even when we went 12-0 up, I didn't think that we were certainly going to win. Thackeray was playing well and we knew that he was always a danger. Widnes had a strong bench, so we knew that they would have the stamina for the full match. When it got to the hour mark, I was thinking "what's going on? We've fallen behind." The time had gone past very quickly, and then Alex Brown scored and that gave us some hope. I wasn't looking at the clock, but I knew that we didn't have much time left, but I thought that we could still do it.

I could feel the atmosphere change and I could sense that Widnes were starting to worry and lose a bit of composure. They had seemed pretty comfortable when they were nine points in front, but once Alex got his first try, Widnes started to panic a bit. We had them under pressure in their own half and they were finding it difficult to get out.

We showed plenty of composure in that set that led up to the try. What a lot of the crowd didn't realise was that the ball was really slippery, like a bar of soap, because the grass was wet and it was humid, so it was difficult to hold on to the ball and very easy to drop it. That kick by Gazz was outstanding. It was right on the spot for Alex Brown and the way that Alex got up and caught that slippery ball and the twisted to ground it was fantastic. Shaun Ainscough was a strong player, but he couldn't match Alex, who really wanted to get that ball and he did.

I'd had to come off before the end because I'd torn may shoulder. I'd done it at Leigh but I'd had painkiller injections because I didn't want to miss the game. Anyway, I felt it go in a tackle and I knew that I couldn't carry on, so I was on the side line when that last try scored and I couldn't really see what had happened until it came up on the screen and then I knew it was a try and that we were going to win. It was an amazing feeling and an amazing day.

Danny Maun

It's not over yet

Widnes were a class side, so we knew that if we went ahead, they would come back at us and we had to have that attitude so that we would be able to fight back. The main thing was that we played till the last minute and even though we didn't have much time left after Alex Brown had scored his first try, we knew that we could do it and that we would get a chance. That's the attitude that you have to have, because if you go behind in a close match and you're thinking that you're not going to be able to win, then you won't. This final went down to the last big play for us. Everyone believed that we'd be able to get the job done and we got the chance to do it. That kick by

Gareth Moore was off the cuff. He saw that there was a chance and he took it. Alex Brown was a good try scorer. He didn't miss many opportunities and he showed that in the final. All he needed was a chance. We could create those opportunities and Alex or Jonny Campbell would get on the end of them and finish them off. When Alex went up and caught that ball, I had no doubt that he'd got it down because he didn't miss those sort of opportunities.

When Alex went over, there were euphoric scenes, but I said to Gareth that it wasn't over yet. I told him to take as much time as was allowed for the kick and then I got the team together and said that we had to make sure that we got the ball from the Widnes kick-off and then it was just one more big effort to get down their end and secure the game. It was in our hands; and that is what happened. We made sure that they didn't get a chance. We'd had our chance and we'd taken it.

Paul Handforth

I wanted to get back on

When we walked out on the field for the start of the game, the noise was unbelievable. The Batley fans were making the most noise and I was wondering where they had all come from. I was thinking that they should be there every week to support us. They were very vocal, but during the game I was so focused that I wasn't really aware of the crowd.

The match went by really quickly. I think that I played the first twenty minutes and then I came off for an interchange and I was thinking "Off already!" Then I was watching the clock because I wanted to get back on. I was living every minute of it with the lads and then it was great to get back on the field with them. We'd got off to a good start, but we knew that Widnes would come back at us, but we just got on with it. When there were errors there was no criticism, no 'bagging' of the players who'd made the mistakes because that can push them further down. The main thing was to carry on and make sure that you completed the next set of six or made the next six tackles. Karl was like that. He'd tell you if something wasn't good enough but the important thing was to move on from there. Paul Handforth was leading from the front on the field. He was vocal, but you don't need too many of them, you just need a couple of them guiding the team.

When Widnes went ahead, I knew that if we could get back to one score behind them that we could win it because we would never give up and when we did get close to their score, I could feel that they were getting edgy and a bit nervous. I thought that we just need one chance, because we had that belief which we'd had all year. We'd come from behind against good teams and we had that attitude that we could do it. Then Gareth Moore put that kick on a postage stamp for Alex Brown and there was hardly any time left. I remember thinking that we musn't make any mistakes, that we had to keep hold of the ball. I had never gripped a ball so tightly as I did when the clock was ticking down during those last couple of minutes. I could feel myself shaking a bit.

When the final whistle went, it was a feeling of absolute relief. I couldn't believe I was part of it and I was thinking of all the people who weren't there and all the people who'd helped me. We'd had our chance and we'd taken it. Then Preecy was pointing out where relatives were in the crowd and it was just brilliant. The fans were singing and chanting. It was the loudest I had ever heard them.

Kris Lythe

I watch it on DVD to remind myself

The game went by very quickly and I was in the zone, just focused on what we needed to do to win. I wasn't really aware of the crowd because you have to shut that out and keep focused on the game. If you are not doing so well and you're aware of the crowd, that can be a distraction.

When we went behind in the second half, I think that for a while we were trying a bit too hard and getting frustrated. We weren't playing our sets properly, but the I got my first try from a pass from Jonny Campbell. Normally Jonny liked to run with the ball but this time I was following him and I called for it because I was coming up at speed and he gave it to me and I was straight through. Then we started to believe that we could do it and Widnes began to worry. We were doing the tackles and not making mistakes any more.

The final try wasn't a planned move. Gazz was very good at playing off the cuff and he just saw the chance. I hadn't seen him put in that kind of kick before, but it was meant to be and to be honest I can't remember much about scoring the try. I have to watch it on DVD to remind myself. It was just natural instinct to jump for that ball and then twist and get it down.

When I watch it, I think how did I not knock it on?

Alex Brown

We snuffed out attacking moves on their left

As it was with the semi-final, we were the underdogs. I don't think that Widnes took us lightly, but they expected to win. We had that 'never say die' feeling. We had reached the final and it didn't matter that we were the underdogs because we believed that we could win. I remember that in terms of attacking there wasn't much going on on our side of the field. It was more down the left side, but we dug in defensively. Mark (Toohey) was my centre and he was more of a back-rower, but he was there for his defence. He was a very solid defender, so we were able to snuff out attacking moves on their left. In the pack we had experienced players and Jay Walton, so we were pretty solid. I don't think that anyone was thinking about scoring themselves, but we just wanted to make sure that we won. There weren't any opportunities for me, but that didn't matter because there were opportunities for others. Me and Mark concentrated on avoiding mistakes. There wasn't anybody in the team whose ego would get in the way of the whole team's performance.

I remember that the game was a bit scrappy, with some dropped ball and that the pitch at Blackpool was a bit tight. We went into the lead and then Widnes came back at us and got in front, but I never thought that we wouldn't be able to win, even when it was getting close to full time. I knew that we would get a chance and that we had the ability to take it. It was weird. I had this feeling that I knew we were going to win. People might say that you can say that because we did win, but it was real. It was the confidence that we had been building, so it just seemed inevitable when Alex Brown went over for the final try.

We couldn't see for certain that he'd got it down from my side of the field, but we just went by the crowd's reactions and the reactions of the Widnes players. Then it came up on the screen. Alex Brown had already been celebrating and even though that's what players do anyway, I could tell from his reactions that it was genuine. He knew that he had scored and so did the Widnes players.

I was aware that there were more Widnes fans in the crowd, but in the second half it was the Batley fans that you could hear and that added to the excitement and I suppose it was part of that feeling that we were going to win. The fans were desperate for us to win and they believed that we could do it. Once the final whistle had gone, the fans went mad and because Batley has a small fan base, a family feel to it, I could recognise most of the ones I could see because I remembered them from previous games. They had been on a journey with us and this win meant so much to them.

Lee Greenwood

Blow that whistle, for God's sake

Because of that gameplan, me and Lee were more like bystanders at first, so I was a bit gutted at not getting more action, but I realised that it was a means to an end and we all had our part to play. We had to make sure that our defence was strong and that nobody got through us and then we had to run the ball out from defence to give the forwards a rest. Karl made good substitutions at the right time to keep the pressure on.

After we had scored the first try, you could really hear the Batley fans. There were more Widnes fans in the ground, but the Batley fans were making more noise. I noticed the same thing when Batley played Leigh in the Championship Final last September. It does you the world of good when you can hear that support.

When Widnes went in front in the second half, I was thinking that we just have to stay positive and dig in. We had a ten or fifteen minute spell when we were making a few errors, dropping the ball, but we dug deep and I knew that if we worked hard for each other we'd get an opportunity. We got two and we were able to take them.

When Alex went up for that last try I was on the other side of the pitch, so it was nerve wracking waiting for the image to come up on the big screen. From where I was, it didn't look as though he could have avoided going into touch. When the try was given and they kicked off, I was thinking "Blow that whistle, for God's sake!" We went deep into their half and then after some scrappy play there was a scrum and that was it.

Mark Toohey

The mistakes I made weren't crucial

It was a really good performance by the team. I had played and lost in a Northern Rail Cup Final when I was at Castleford, so I was determined not to miss out again.

Most of the players had not had that experience. I can remember that I made a couple of errors because those are the things which stick in your mind. You start off with the mindset that you are not going to make any mistakes, but realistically it's always likely that you will and when you do, they are the things that you remember, not the good stuff that you did.

The mistakes I made weren't crucial in that they didn't have a major impact on the game. Overall, I think that I put in a good performance. I did some good tackling and some hard runs like the rest of the pack. We were all working together and trying to make sure that nobody had to do too much work. It was a real gutsy performance from the team. The backs, wingers and centres, helped to relieve the pressure on the forwards by bringing the ball out of defence.

When the final whistle went I had an enormous feeling of pride and elation. That was for myself, the team and all the fans who'd had to wait so long for Batley to win a major trophy. When I'd played in the final for Castleford, they were the favourites, but we lost. This was the opposite situation and all the better for it. Members of my family were there and some friends as well. My granddad, who's since passed away, was really proud of my achievement.

Byron Smith

Has he dropped it?

We had a massive start to the game. I got a second try after Jay Walton had scored one and that eased us into the game and gave us a boost and helped us to find our feet.

We knew that Widnes would come back at us because they were a good team. That's why they were in the final.

We'd played them earlier and it had been a 30 all draw and that was a tough outing. They had skilful players like Thackeray, so we knew what we were up against, and we were ready for them. They got back into it, as we knew they would, but we didn't wilt. We knew that we would get an opportunity. We were the underdogs and that suited us.

It might be that when Widnes went ahead by more that one score, they thought that's it, but we had overcome Leigh in the semi-final and in a way that was a bigger stepping stone. When Widnes overtook us, we knew it was going to be tough but we felt that if we just stuck to our game then some chances would come, and they did.

Alex's first try was a great move and then he did that fantastic 'salmon' leap to grab the ball from Gazz's kick.

I was off the field at the time and the dugout was on the other side of the pitch from where he scored, so it was impossible to see whether he had got the ball down or whether he had gone into touch. I was peeking at the screen, which was quite small, waiting for the image to come up and it seemed to take forever. The longer it took, I was thinking has he dropped it and although instinctively I thought it was a try, it isn't one until it's been given. Once it was given than I was jumping for joy because I knew that we were going to win.

Sean Hesketh

I managed to dislodge the ball

The game went by very quickly apart from at the end after Alex had scored his second try. I can remember Paddy Hesketh scoring a try, but it was a close game and I think that both teams showed some nervousness because there were mistakes by both sides – basic errors and dropping the ball.

I know we went behind but I can't remember by how many, but I thought that we could still come back and win the game. Before Alex Brown scored his winning try I managed to dislodge the ball from one of their players in a tackle and that gave us a chance to attack their line. When I retired, they did a video for me and the tackle was on it. It was quite emotional for me when Karl Harrison spoke about it at my retirement because he referred to me winning the Northern Rail Cup for him with that tackle. That final try made it special because we had a chance to win the cup and we took it.

When Alex's try was sent to the video ref it seemed to take ages. When it was given we all had eyes on the clock, though we weren't supposed to be doing that. We knew that we could hold out and avoid mistakes. I seem to remember that someone picked up the ball and more or less stuffed it up his jumper. He made sure that there was no chance of him losing it. The main thing was that we stayed switched on and the experienced players made sure that we did.

Once the final whistle went, in some ways we didn't know what to do. We were just jumping on one another. It was madness and the crowd were going wild as well. You could feel how excited they were. My parents were there. I spotted them in the crowd and gave them a wave. I don't remember much happening in the changing rooms because I think that we just wanted to get showered and get a beer.

Tommy Gallagher

A question of who would make a crucial mistake

The game itself flew by and even though we went behind in the second half we always felt that we were in it. We knew that it was going to be a tight game and it was a question of who would make a crucial mistake or do something special. We never lost confidence and we just kept at it. Karl always emphasised that we needed to do the simple things accurately – passing the ball, tackling and running hard. We kept a pretty solid defence even though we did make some mistakes. I think Tommy made a difference when he came on because he took it to Widnes and did some tackles that shook them up. In the end it took a bit of magic from Gareth Moore and Alex Brown, but we had earned it by staying in the game.

When Alex scored, I was off the field so from where I was it looked as though it could go either way. There are not many players who could have done what Alex did, leaping up and twisting to get the ball down.

John Gallagher

I had played it out too much in my head

When we came out, I tried to block out the crowd and stay focused on the game. Whilst we were in the changing room I was nervous and excited, but on the field the atmosphere was electric. It was great to see the supporters who had been so loyal to the club and family members as well. It was a special moment to see spectators who'd been watching Batley all their lives and this was the first chance they'd had to see their team in a major final. The fans help to pay your wages and you want to give them something back. I could hear some shouting my name but I tried to stay focused on the game.

I don't think that I had my best game in the final, perhaps because I had played it out in my head too much before the game. It was good that we went in front because that helped to settle our nerves, but we knew that Widnes were good enough to come back at us and they did. We bombed a few chances and missed some tackles but then we started to build pressure and keep them in their own half. Jonny Campbell did some good returns from kicks and made Widnes work hard. Karl Harrison drummed it into us that we needed to play the game in their half as much as possible; keep them within thirty metres of their line so that they had a kick of seventy metres or more to reach our try line.

When Alex jumped for that ball, I was right beside him and I couldn't believe that he'd been able to get up and then twist to get over the line. What a finish! There was about two minutes to go after the kick, so I was a bit nervous because we'd lost games in the last minute in the past, but we manged to take the ball to their line and that was it. When the final whistle went, it felt like a dream, like it wasn't real, the atmosphere and everything about it.

Ash Lindsay

It was an easy match to referee

What I remember most about the 2010 Northern Rail Cup Final is that it was a tremendous game; a see-saw game that was one of the best matches of that season. Batley went into an early lead and then Widnes struck back. Once they built a lead, I think they thought that the game was won, but then their concentration lapsed and they made an error and surrendered possession to Batley which led to Batley scoring a try.

As I recall, it was a very good try scored by Alex Brown and with the conversion that put Batley just three points behind Widnes with ten minutes to go. The final try by Alex Brown was quite spectacular. It was clear that Widnes couldn't shake Batley off and that Batley would probably get one more chance. They did and they took it when Alex Brown leapt in the air and grabbed the ball.

I sent it up to the video ref, Richard Silverwood, but back then we didn't have to give a preliminary ruling. It was just up to the video ref. If I had been required to make a preliminary ruling, I would have said it was a try because it looked as though he had got the ball down cleanly.

I remember it was a nice warm day and, though it had rained heavily during the morning, it was dry during the match with a bit of a breeze. It was an easy match to referee. I didn't need to get involved very much apart from the standard interventions. It was a very good competitive game that was played in a good spirit.

That was usually the case with both Batley and Widnes.

Robert Hicks (match referee)

It might have been ruled a foul now

The game was a bit topsy turvy. We went ahead and then we were behind because we got a bit soft and let them in. Even behind I was still confident we could win, that we had the ability to do it. It was a question of whether we had enough time, or whether we'd be beaten by the clock. In the end it was two brilliant moves that did it for us.

It was a brilliant Jonny Campbell pass that set Alex Brown up for his first try. Alex ran a great line, but the pass allowed him to do that. Johnny isn't usually a passer, he's a runner, but that was really great. Tommy Gallagher also came up with two massive plays that enabled us to build pressure in the Widnes half, which is just what you want.

Everybody thinks about the Gareth Moore kick that led to the Alex Brown try as the event that won us the game, but from a coach's point of view it was that tackle by Tommy Gallagher that won us the game. It might have been ruled a foul now because he hit the ball just with his shoulder, but that tackle had to be made and he made it and we got the ball back near their line and the rest is history

That little chip by Gareth Moore wasn't rehearsed, he just did it. He played what was in front of him. Alex Brown was a big athletic player, quite a bit taller than Shaun Ainscough, who was a bit of a midget, if we can say that. Most of our kicks did go that way, but this time we were set up to go right but he sent it left. We created an opportunity on the short side, but we had four on the short side which was too many to run the ball, so Gareth put it in the air. Alex used his athletic ability to get hold of the ball and get it down. As soon as I saw it I jumped up because I thought he had done it.

There was a *Yorkshire Post* journalist behind me who was looking at a TV monitor and he said "I think he's got it Karl."

Gareth hit the post, but he should have got it, even though it was from the touchline. There was a bit of a delay before the try was confirmed and I think that it helped us because it meant that we had time to settle down from the excitement and then we just had a couple of minutes left.

Karl Harrison

It made me light headed

I know that Karl was confident that we could win. We'd beaten Leigh, so we could beat Widnes and we did. I think that Karl gave Gareth Moore a bit of a telling off at half-time for doing that drop goal, but in the end that made the difference. At the end, with my family there and my parents, it was fantastic. The sheer excitement when Alex Brown scored that winning try and then hearing the final whistle made me light headed. Kevin Nicholas was in tears because it meant so much to him. It was hard to take it all in, but we'd done it.

Paul Harrison (Chief Executive, Batley RLFC)

I'm still anxious when I watch it on DVD

When we scored two early tries and went into the lead a lot of people around me were getting excited, but I was trying to stay calm. I was saying that there was still a lot of time left in the game, so we shouldn't get too carried away because anything could happen.

Widnes were red hot favourites amongst the press, but they were trailing. Just before half-time, Gareth Moore dropped a goal that, in the end, proved to be the winner. Some fans were complaining that Moore had surrendered an attacking position by dropping the goal, but I was happy that Batley had come away with some points.

After half-time, when Widnes fought back and went into a nine point lead, I felt that we might have missed our chance.

I thought we were trying too hard and needed to relax, which is what we did when Alex Brown went over for his first try and then there was a sense of inevitability that we would get another. In fact, I said to my son when we were nine points behind that if we could get another try we would go on to win the game. He was saying "We're not going to do it, Dad", and we did.

When Alex Brown got his first try there was nobody who could have stopped him; he was too powerful, and then we were on a roll. That try turned the match back in our favour and you could see that Widnes were rattled because they realised that the momentum had switched. When I watch it again on DVD and it gets to the last ten minutes, I am still anxious and shaking even though I know how it's going to turn out.

What a try it was. When Gareth Moore put up the kick, the ball seemed to be in the air for an eternity; and what a leap and a great take. Alex knew he'd scored. We were at the opposite side of the field, so we couldn't see whether Alex had got the ball down but we could tell from his reaction and the reaction of the players around him that he knew that he'd scored. The expression on Alex's face as he was walking back was something to behold.

When Widnes kicked off I think that it was Tommy Gallagher who caught the ball and it couldn't have gone to a better person, because you knew that he was going to make sure that the ball was secure there were only a couple of minutes left in the game. It's all a bit of a blur after that, apart from a recollection that Widnes knocked on near their own line and the game was effectively over because there wasn't time to complete the scrum.

That was it. Batley had won.

There was a lot of crying and disbelief. I remember leaning on the balcony at the front of the stand and breathing heavily. There was no better way to win a trophy; coming from behind and scoring the winning try two minutes from time. The two Alex Brown tries were great tries as well.

They weren't lucky tries, they were the result of skilful play. The way in which Alex Brown twisted his body as he came down from the leap was brilliant. If a try like that had been scored in a Super League match, the commentators would have been showing it every week.

When Alex Brown moved on from Batley he never quite developed into the player many people thought he would become. In fact, when he played against Batley, he never caused us any trouble. I think he was very happy playing for Batley and perhaps moved on too soon. Anyway, he will always be remembered for those two tries in the second half.

John Miller (Director, Batley RLFC)

Premature celebrations and a charge for the medals

When Alex Brown scored his first try with about twelve minutes to go, I thought that we could score again, but I wasn't sure if we had enough time. I knew that the team would have the determination to get another try, but it was just a question of whether they had enough time. We were on a roll and I could see that Widnes were edgy. When Alex Brown went over for the try, we could not see for certain that he'd got the ball down because there were Widnes players on top of him, but it looked as though he had. When the try was awarded and we were in front on the scoreboard, I knew that we had won because there wasn't enough time for Widnes to score. There were about two minute left when Widnes kicked off after the try, but I was confident that we would keep the ball safe.

During the match we were on a balcony and there were some steps in the middle separating us from the Widnes directors and my abiding memory of the game is that with five minutes to go (we were three points behind) a lady from the RFL was signalling for me to go down pitch side for the end of the match. I refused to go until the final whistle had been blown because in order to get down to the pitch I would have had to go down the steps and then through a tunnel onto the pitch, so I would have lost sight of the action on the pitch for a short while and I didn't want to miss anything because I felt we could score again.

My wife, Bev, and Sue Winner nudged me and drew my attention to the Widnes directors and wives on the other side of the steps. They were hugging each other and shaking hands because they thought that they had won. The chairman went down the steps and then eventually came skipping out of the tunnel onto the pitch, but by the time he had got there Alex Brown had scored his second try whilst the Widnes chairman had been en route from the balcony. He had missed the try. When he set off down the steps Widnes were winning but by the time he got pitch side, they were losing by one point and there was hardly any time left in the game.

The Widnes chairman had a face like thunder because he had

assumed that he was going down to the pitch to celebrate his team's victory. He wasn't arrogant, though. As soon as I got down to the pitch he shook my hand straight away and congratulated me.

He was absolutely distraught because he had thought that they were going to win the Cup. It must have been hard for him, but he didn't take it out on us. I was a bit tearful and I was hugging Karl. The team then went to get their medals, which we had to pay for. We got some extra ones because we wanted every member of the squad to have one, not just the 17 who had played on the day. I was surprised because I didn't expect us to have to pay for the medals.

The cost was deducted from our share of the gate and it was the same for Widnes. I think each medal cost about £20-£30. The medals were about the size of an egg. There might be a record of the deduction from the money we received as our share of the gate.

Kevin Nicholas (Chairman, Batley RLFC)

I get all wound up and tense

The first thing to say is that when I go to a game that's really important for Batley, even if I go with a group of people, I don't want to sit with them. I want to be by myself because I get all wound up and tense and I don't want to talk to anybody.

More than anything else, I remember the last kick of the game, when Alex Brown went up above Shaun Ainscough, grabbed the ball and scored. The Batley fans went absolutely crackers. I ran onto the pitch, even though the steward told me not to, but I didn't take any notice. I ran over to Danny Maun, who had a bad shoulder, and without thinking, I banged him on the shoulder and then I threw my Batley scarf round his neck, so any shots of Danny wearing a scarf at the end of the match, it's my scarf that I threw round his neck.

Talking about that final kick, one of my mates was saying that it was a planned move. I don't think it was a planned move. I mean they would have practised kicks, but not necessarily that particular move. It was the last kick of the game, in play. After the game I asked if I could go up to see the players. I saw Tiger Handforth, the

Gallagher brothers. They were all chuffed to bits. Mick Stephenson was there and he's on one of the photos I took.

John McVeigh (fan)

Red and white flags and obscured view

We had those big red and white chequered flags. I've still got them in the garage.

John Cresswell (fan)

There were a number of fans with red and white chequered flags who were blocking my view. I would have ripped one of them up if I could have got hold of one. Every time there was some crucial action, one of those flags was obstructing my view.

David Hopkin (fan)

Excellent view of the pitch

We were up at the back of the stand about midway between the 20 metre line and the halfway line. We had an excellent view of the pitch. There was one section where all the TV cameras were and they had taken out all the seats because they were in the process of improving the ground because the Blackpool football team had been promoted to the Premier League.

Grahame Hobson (fan)

I was ringing home on my mobile

The thing I remember most, and this is probably the same for lots of fans, is when Alex Brown jumped above 'Ainy' (Shaun Ainscough), caught the ball and scored the winning try. Afterwards, I remember that one of the commentators on the TV or the radio said something like "Alex Brown leapt like a salmon out of the water!" I remember that the try had to be reviewed by the video ref in order to check whether Alex Brown was onside and had got the ball down properly. We were behind the sticks at the end where he scored but it was on the opposite side of the sticks to where we were, so we didn't know for certain that the try was going to be given. I was really nervous watching the replay on the big screen and I was ringing home on my mobile, asking them whether they could see on the replay that it was a try. I was asking if they could see if Alex had got the ball down cleanly. I don't know how long it took to make the decision, but it seemed like a really long time before the try was awarded. It felt like we were waiting ten minutes for the decision.

As soon as the try was awarded, the crowd went wild and there were a few pint glasses spilt as fans threw their arms in the air without thinking that they had a pint of beer in one hand. I think that I'd had a full pint but there was only half of it left. A lot of beer ended up on the floor. Some people got onto the pitch because there weren't enough police and stewards to stop them.

Richard Drake (fan)

I was screaming at the telly

I watched the game on the TV and at half-time I thought that we were not going to win. I wasn't expecting Batley to win; hoping that they would but not expecting it. I just wanted them to put in a good performance. The last 10 minutes were fantastic, absolutely brilliant. When Brown jumped over the top of Ainscough to get that try, I couldn't believe it. There was only two minutes to go and Widnes had to kick off to us. My wife wondered what the noise was when Brown scored that try because I was screaming at the telly. She thought that I'd gone mad. She said "What's up with you?"

Keith Frankland (fan)

Increased heart rate

From where we were in the stand, on the opposite side of the field to where Alex Brown scored, it looked touch and go as to whether he had stayed in play. It seemed to take ages for the video ref to make a decision and my heart was going fifty to the dozen.

Peter Homer (fan)

Gracious Widnes fans

We sat in the main stand at Bloomfield Road and we mixed with the Widnes fans. They were really good at the end of the match. They shook hands with us and said that we deserved to win even though they must have been really disappointed to let in that last try. I take my hat off to them. You know, they wished us all the best.

Barry Lee (fan)

A steely determination and rapid action

When the teams came out onto the pitch for the start of the match, the Widnes players were strutting like cocks but there was a steely determination on the faces of the Batley players. We were in front early on, but when Widnes came back and took the lead, I thought that was it but then we came back and scored ten points in the last ten minutes or so. When Gareth Moore put that chip kick up and Alex Brown leapt up above Shaun Ainscough and went over the line, we were not sure whether he had scored because there was a load of bodies around the try line.

When you are watching live at the ground, the action happens very quickly and you are not seeing it in close-up like you might be on telly. They went to the screen to check whether it was a try and it seemed to be ages before they made the decision. Everyone went mental and all the Batley fans were screaming and cheering, but then Widnes had to kick-off back to us because there was still a couple of minutes left. It was still tense though because although right at the end Widnes knocked on and there was a scrum, we knocked on from the scrum and we were thinking "Oh No!" and the fans were groaning, wanting the final whistle to be blown because there was only one point in it. There was countdown from 10 and even that seemed to take an eternity. Then the final whistle blew and I remember that Tiger Handforth ran to the end where the Batley supporters were and fell to his knees in front of us. It was fantastic.

John McGowan (fan and ex-player)

Expletive not deleted

As Alex Brown was catching the ball my mobile rang. It was my friend Alister Williams, who was on holiday, asking "how are we doing?" In that moment he (Alex Brown) touched down and all hell broke loose!! I replied "we've fucking well won" ... the phone went dead. I sat down, took it all in and started shedding a tear, wishing my Dad, who was no longer with us, could have been there, having watched Batley all his life. He would have loved that moment.

On the way home the phone rang and it was Alister. "I take it we won" he said and then explained that he had Susan and daughter in the car ... whoops ... and that I'll be forever known as "Colin we've fucking well won Bottomley!

Colin Bottomley (fan)

I still feel the same excitement

As I wasn't a Batley fan, I knew the names of more of the Widnes players than Batley. I knew the names of a few of the Batley players, but when Batley went into the lead with two early tries, I was rooting for them. Later, Batley fell behind and then I thought that they weren't going to do it but in the end they pulled it off. I've watched the match time and again on the internet and I am just as excited as I was on the day during the last 10 minutes or so when Batley were still nine points behind, even though I know how it turns out.

It brings back memories of just what a great occasion it was. When I watch Alex Brown leaping to catch that kick from Gareth Moore I still feel the same excitement as when I was watching it live. It was like he had springs in his boots and he just rose up above the defender and caught the ball. The crowd went absolutely mad because it was so close to the end of the match and that try put us in front. It seemed like a long time before the try was confirmed and it was a bit nerve wracking while we waited, but when it was awarded the fans were jumping up and down and screaming and yelling.

Allan Waite (fan of Bradford Bulls)

Not my usual self

Being a Batley fan at the Northern Rail Cup final, unlike at normal league matches, I was cheering everything we did. Normally, I would be fairly taciturn watching a game, not wanting to draw attention to myself, but at Blackpool I was carried along by the enthusiasm of the spectators. I'm usually fairly reserved, but not on this occasion. The feeling generated by the crowd is infectious and ultimately it takes over and makes you behave differently.

There was a lot of toing and frowing in the game as Batley went ahead and then Widnes overhauled them and at that point I thought that Batley were probably going to lose by a few points, so I was feeling a bit disappointed. Then with about ten minutes to go Alex Brown scored a try and with the conversion we were only three points behind, so it seemed possible for us to win. That's when it got really exciting, but I still didn't think that we were going to manage it. Then with a few minutes to go Gareth Moore put the ball up in the air in the corner and Alex Brown leapt in the air above the Widnes player and grabbed the ball and scored. It was madness after that. It seemed quite a long time before the try was confirmed.

We were diagonally opposite where Alex had scored, so we couldn't see for certain that he had touched it down, but we were fairly certain that it would'nt be disallowed because of offside because we could see a line of Batley players, including Alex Brown, who seemed to be behind the kicker. After it had been awarded, I wasn't sure how much time was left. I knew there wasn't very much, but I was still thinking I hope we don't give away a penalty because we were only one point ahead. I was thinking 'It's never over till it's over.' Then when the final whistle blew, there was complete elation. When we went back to the Director's suite there were Widnes people there and they congratulated us.

I can't remember how I acquired it, but I came away from the game with a Widnes tie. Some Widnes fan must have given it to me, but I can't remember the circumstances.

Stuart Merton (fan)

I was nearly crushed

Batley supporters were outnumbered by Widnes fans. When Batley dropped a goal before half-time there were some supporters who were asking why they had done that. Well, by the end of the match, when we won by one point, they got the answer to that question.

I had a pint at half-time because my throat was dry from all the shouting and cheering. It wasn't until the final minute that I was confident we were going to win. Alex Brown had scored and we were only one point in front but the play was right up at the Widnes end. The game had been tense as Batley and Widnes seemed to take it in turns to go into the lead. When we were nine points behind and there wasn't much time left on the clock, I was thinking that we were not going to be able to do it. Then the ball went up in the corner with just a few minutes to go and Alex Brown seemed to get up really high, well above the defender. He caught the ball cleanly and then as he was coming down he twisted so that he could get the ball over the line. It seemed as though he must have had something in his boots to enable him to leap so high. The stand behind the posts erupted, then that spread to the Batley fans who were elsewhere. Then for the last couple of minutes it was 'squeaky bum' time.

When the final whistle blew, the fans on the terraces went wild. I was nearly crushed in the rush to the barriers as fans wanted to get onto the pitch' I remember that I turned and looked up to where the directors were and I swear that I saw Kevin (Nicholas) in tears. Also, I've never seen fans of the losing team empty the stands so quickly. They didn't wait for their team to come and get their medals. The Widnes fans were very quiet, but I suppose that's not surprising because they had been in the lead with only a few minutes to go. We stayed for the presentation of the cup which took place on the field.

I won't forget the look on Kevin's face; it was a mixture of joy, surprise and satisfaction. The team brought the cup to where the Batley fans were so that the fans could touch the cup and there was massive applause for the players.

Billy Lonergan (fan)

Widnes ribbons on the cup

I remember that they gave the Man of the Match award to Thackeray because they made the decision about five minutes before the end of the game, whereas if they had waited a few more minutes they might have given it to Alex Brown. They had to change the ribbons on the cup because they had tied the Widnes ribbons on. It just shows you that you need to wait until the end of the match, if the score is close.

Ged Littlewood (fan)

Unreasonable stewards

The stewards at Blackpool were horrible to us. All we wanted to do was to was to go and congratulate the lads. We hadn't won a major trophy in ages, but they treated us as though we were soccer hooligans. John McVeigh took no notice of what the police said. He jumped over the barrier and ran across the field to congratulate the Batley players. He said that he didn't care and nobody was going to stop him. There was one little steward who was especially horrible to us, so we were telling him that Karl Harrison will sort you out and that he'd be singing a different tune once Karl came along.

When we went round to the changing rooms to wait for the players to come out and give them a big cheer, there were mounted police there. I don't think that they had any idea that rugby league crowds were different from football fans.

Ged Littlewood (fan)

I missed Alex Brown's try

I had to buy the DVD in order to see Alex Brown's winning try and I'll tell you why. We were sitting just to the right of the tunnel where the players came out and when he had scored the first try ten minutes from the end and then it was getting towards full-time, I turned away from the action and I dropped my head onto John

Atkin's shoulder and said "We're going to be the nearly men again!" because we were still three points behind and there were only about two minutes to go. Suddenly I heard an incredible roar and when I looked up, I had just missed Alex Brown scoring, but the Batley fans were going wild. Of course, we had to wait for the try to be confirmed by the video ref and it seemed to take ages. After missing that try I didn't come round for four years. What a moment to miss! Anyway, I've got it on DVD, so I can re-watch it when I want to.

Steve Pickard (fan)

A sweaty moment

After the match had finished, Alex Brown came over to talk to his wife at the railings, so I went down and patted him on the back to congratulate him and as a result I got covered in a shower of sweat because I had forgot that he would be sweating at the end of the game, particularly after what he had done.

Steve Pickard (fan)

Cheer up, you've won

When we got back to the limo, there was only David Harrison's dad missing and he was the oldest amongst us. You would have thought that it would have been the youngest that we'd end up waiting for. Apparently, he gone up to the boardroom after the match because he knew someone who was in there. We waited quite a while for him to turn up and whilst we were waiting, we were saying "What shall we do?" We were getting a bit worried and some Widnes fans who saw us said "Cheer up, you've won!"

Steve Pickard (fan)

On edge most of the time

I think I had got the tickets through the post and we were in the stand with other Batley fans, but it was freezing because it was out of the sun. The Widnes fans were in the sun, which I thought was a bit unfair. I was so tense and nervous during the match that I didn't really enjoy it. I was on edge most of the time, especially since we went into an early lead with a couple of tries and then they overhauled us. I was just so nervous that, although it was an exciting match, it was not an enjoyable experience for me until the final few minutes. There was too much tension. Gareth Moore dropped a goal before half time and that was really important in the end because that made the difference between us and Widnes. When Widnes were in the lead at half-time, it was too much for me, especially when they went further ahead in the second half. Even when Alex Brown scored his first try with about ten minutes to go, I didn't think that we would be able to win because I didn't think that there was enough time left. When Alex Brown jumped in the air and grabbed the ball and went over the try line, I was cheering like hell. I couldn't believe it, especially because it was so near the end of the game. Alex Brown was like Churchill, it was his finest hour. We were on the opposite side to the one where he scored the try, so we weren't 100% certain that he'd got the ball down, but it looked as though he had. Then when it came up on the big screen , you could clearly see that he had scored and we just went wild, cheering and jumping about.

Barry Dale (fan)

I like to move about

I travelled to Blackpool on the coach and I started off behind the posts with other Batley fans and gradually gravitated to the side terrace where there were a few more of our lot. I don't like to stand in one place for the whole of the game. I like to move about and maybe chat to different people. You also get a different view of what's going on. You can take in the atmosphere.

When we got a couple of tries and went into the lead, it was looking good, but then Widnes came back at us and their forwards were bullying us, but we didn't give in we stuck to it. Paul Handforth was good. Karl had brought him to the club and he made a difference. He helped to keep the team going. He had a good dummy and he could pick a pass. That helped to keep the team moving and

Gareth Moore had a good kicking game. He dropped that goal and maybe some supporters were wondering why he'd done it, but in the end it made the difference. It was a great pass from Jonny Campbell when Alex Brown got his first try. You could sense his determination as he went through. You could see that the players thought that they could win after that. They just needed another chance and you could see that Widnes were a bit shocked. Then Gareth Moore put that kick up in the corner and, of course, it was Shaun Ainscough up against Alex Brown and Alex just leapt up like a gazelle.

It took some doing to get that ball and get it down. I was thinking "he's done it, and that's it," but there were a couple of minutes left after the kick. We kept them down at their end and didn't give them much of a chance, but my nerves were jangling a bit. I've supported Batley for a long time and I was at the Yorkshire Cup Final in 1952, when Batley lost to Huddersfield in the fog. I'd waited a long time for Batley to be in an important final again.

Malcom Westerby (fan)

Tears galore

What a day, what a game; cried lots of tears through the game thinking we were going to lose; then very happy tears at the end; will never forget this moment in Batley Bulldogs' history.

Irene Fletcher (fan)

He was covering his back

We were right at the end of the stand, near where it met the terrace behind the post, so we were on the opposite side to where Alex Brown scored his final try, but we were more or less in line with the try line and there were plenty of Batley fans around us because they were mainly concentrated at that end.

I was watching the game with more of a player's eye rather than that of a coach because I wasn't directly involved in coaching at Championship level. The game was very much a roller coaster affair. We got off to a very good start, with a couple of tries, but then they hit back and overtook us and at that point I thought that Widnes would probably go on to win the trophy. Then, when Alex Brown scored his first try, I thought that Batley could now give it a good go. They didn't have a lot of time, but I thought it was Batley's game to win and Widnes's game to lose.

I could see that the Widnes players were getting more edgy and nervous once Batley were only three points behind. We had a decent view of that last try and my initial response to my mate was that Alex Brown had got the ball down. The reaction from both sets of players seemed to indicate that Alex had scored. Robert Hicks went to the video referee, which was only natural because in such a big game the ref would not want to award a winning try that was later shown to have been a poor decision. Quite rightly, he was covering his back.

Craig Lingard (fan and ex-player)

A typical dour Yorkshireman

Dad went to the final with his partner, Iris, and we met them at the ground in Blackpool. As a Batley fan, if Batley were obviously going to lose the game, my dad had a habit of leaving the ground ten minutes before the end of the game. He would just say "Right, I'm off" and he'd be on his way.

When the final hooter went at Blackpool and Batley had won their first major trophy since 1924 and the first major trophy my dad had seen them win, I felt a tap on my shoulder and when I, in an exultant mood, turned round, my dad said that he had to go because he had only paid for three hours in the car park and the time was up, so he didn't stay for the presentation of the trophy. But that was very typical of my dad. He was a typical dour Yorkshireman.

Adrian Wales (fan)

It's the hope that gets you

When Batley were behind at half-time, I thought that we would probably lose and then even when Alex Brown scored his first try, I didn't want to think Batley would win because the disappointment would be too great if they lost. I didn't dare to dream, as they say. As Adrian Chiles pointed out, it's not the disappointment that gets you, it's the hope! Anyway, it was an incredible day and we had a good view of Alex Brown's final dramatic try, after which I knew that we were going to win.

Adrian Wales (fan)

We didn't have to convert the final try

We must have got to the ground at about 3:15pm for the four o'clock kick-off and we were in the stand on the touchline, on the same side where Alex Brown scored the winning try. I had high hopes that we could win, but it was probably more a case of my heart saying that we could win and my head thinking that we would probably lose. The match seemed to go by very quickly as we got two early tries and then Widnes came back at us, which I knew they would. When Gareth Moore dropped a goal before half-time I was wondering why he'd done that because we were pressing them, but as it turned out, that was a crucial goal because it meant that he didn't have to convert the final try for us to be in the lead. When Widnes scored a couple of tries and went ahead in the second half, I thought that it was settled, until Alex Brown scored his first try and after the kick we were only three points behind. That's when I started to think that we might be able to do it, and I was hoping that we had enough time. I could see that Widnes were getting a bit rattled and were starting to lose their composure a bit. It was just a question of whether we could get another chance in the time that was left. I remember that most of the play in the last five minutes or so was down at their end.

We were able to see Alex Brown go up for the ball but we couldn't see whether he got it down, although it looked as though he had. Once it came up on the screen it was obvious that he had scored and the whole place erupted. It brought a tear to the eye because we knew that we had won and we were jumping about and going mad – what a feeling, especially after all those years of supporting Batley and not seeing them win anything important.

Mick Bedford (fan)

In the brace position

My friend couldn't stand the tension. He couldn't watch the game in those last few minutes. He had his face in his hands, like he was in the brace position in a plane and he was shaking. When the final whistle went we were jumping up and down and I took my shirt off and I was swinging it around.

Darren Rhodes (fan, mankini man)

The response in the press

As might be expected, there was a very generous response in the local press to Batley's unexpected success. The coverage blended reports of the match itself with personal stories about individual experiences on the day of the Northern Rail Cup Final. Dave Craven, writing in the Yorkshire Post, *19th July, 2010, paid tribute to the way in which Batley, on one of the smallest budgets in the Championship, had been able to defy the odds: "Batley created one last chance when a fearsome tackle saw Flynn spill in front of his own posts, epitomising the energy and passion Harrison's side showed throughout. Despite their underdog status, a performance rich in character was rewarded at the death."*

This observation chimes with Karl Harrison's testimony that Tommy Gallagher's tackle was as important as Alex Brown's spectacular leap because it gave Batley the chance that they needed. The article also noted that Batley now had the right to apply to join Super League, but framed it within the context of Karl Harrison's response to a question about whether Batley would proceed with a Super League application, in which Karl said: "I'm going to write it myself in the Frontier club on the back of a beer mat. I'll post it to the RFL chief executive, Nigel Wood, tomorrow morning. We've no ambitions to go in Super League. We're happy to stay in the Championship and that's what Batley's about."

The Batley News, *22nd July, 2010, focused on the personal experiences of particular fans. Under the heading "Batley victory is icing on cake", there was a story about John and Janet Virr, who were due to celebrate their thirty third wedding anniversary on the 23rd July, 2010, and for whom Batley's victory was a fitting present. The newspaper also included a story about the winners of the Batley News ticket competition, one of whom was Jean Dennis who came onto the pitch at half-time with her three-month-old grandson, Alistair Moir. Apparently, this was not the first time Alistair had been to a Batley match, having been taken to one when he was only three weeks old. The article noted that Alistair, wearing a specially made cup final shirt, slept through most of the second half, despite the noise from the crowd.*

The Spenborough Guardian, *23rd July, 2010, highlighted Paul Cullen's (Widnes coach) gracious response to Batley's last ditch victory: "Credit to the Batley players. We knew they were a tough and resilient team. We have known that all season. A play like that for Brown's second try deserves to win a final. It was an outstanding kick, an even better catch and it broke our hearts."*

This newspaper also included a quote from a Batley fan, Paul Hopkins, who was at the game with five members of his family, including his father, Frank, who had been at the Yorkshire Cup Final in 1952 when Batley lost to Huddersfield: "That was a day and a half! I was quite stunned, almost in shock. I was very confident, but I've supported Batley all my life and I'm 53 now, but I have been let down so many times before. I took the day off work on Monday and watched it twice and both times I wasn't convinced we were going to win!"

5.

TEAM SPIRIT AND DETERMINATION

The reasons why Batley confounded the pundits

AS WITH DEWSBURY's 1973 Championship triumph, there are a number of interconnected reasons why Batley, as clear underdogs, were able to confound the pundit' predictions in 2010. Some of these reasons, including the role of the coach, have already been hinted at in the preceding testimony.

Karl Harrison was a different, though no less effective coach, compared to Tommy Smales, but, like Tommy, Karl was massively important in the creation of a wonderful team spirit which enabled Batley to defeat teams which, player for player, seemed to be stronger than Batley.

At the same time, we should not underestimate the defensive and creative qualities of Batley's players, qualities which help to explain their very convincing victory against Leigh in the semi-final of the Northern Rail.

The Heavy Woollen Victories

They were such a close outfit

We won because we were totally focused on the game and that is what is needed for a coach to get the best out of a team. We had a team of locals. There was only Govin and Toothill who were Lancastrians, whilst the rest were locals.

They were such a close outfit and they all wanted to play for each other and that came through in that final when we came back from behind to win the game.

Karl Harrison

Groundwork already laid

Some of the people who had gone before me had laid the groundwork. Gary Thornton and David Ward had both done well. When I started as coach at Batley, I got the full backing of the board. We were short of a good half-back, so Kevin brought in Paul Handforth, who was one of our best signings. He could run a game.

Karl Harrison

You need a bit of luck

Well, I think that some of it was to do with the coaching. Karl had instilled belief into the players that they were good enough to win the Northern Rail Cup.

They developed the belief that other teams would have to be at their best to beat us. Obviously, you also need a bit of luck. Alex Brown's final try was fantastic. A great kick and a marvellous jump to grab the ball and twist, but on another day it might not quite have worked. It was as though we were destined to win.

We'd built a team, not just a group of individual players. Everyone at the club is important and they all had to believe in the model. It's a team effort because it's a team game. We had a blend of the right players and that's what we aim for.

Paul Harrison (Chief Executive, Batley RLFC)

A good blend of players

I knew that we had a chance because we had Tiger, Sean Hesketh, Jonny Campbell and Ash Lindsay, all of whom on their day could match Widnes. Player for player, Widnes had the better team. Also, it wasn't that long since they had been in Super League.

However, I think that we had the better team as a whole. All the players worked for each other and they gelled. We had a good blend of experienced players, young players and some players who had a bit of an edge. They were the ones who would get stuck in no matter what and if it got a bit dirty, so much the better as far as they were concerned. Alex Brown was only twenty two, but he was on fire when he was at Batley, out on loan from Huddersfield.

Gareth Moore was also young and very cocky. He had a swagger about him even though he looked as though he was still a schoolboy.

John Miller (Director, Batley RLFC)

Never say die attitude

We never gave up, as the Widnes chairman would testify. I still wonder what he must have felt like when he came out onto the field and realised that Widnes were now losing and there were only two minutes of the game left to play.

Kevin Nicholas (Chairman, Batley RLFC)

He got rid of a few 'bad eggs'

Karl Harrison used to call me 'suntan' and you knew that if he said that you'd done alright (with that big horrible face), you must have had a really good game. He was brilliant. He got the best out of the players; he challenged you and he would drop you if you weren't good enough.

Nobody believed that we could do it, apart from the directors, the coach and the team. We had a good mix of new and experienced players. Jonny Campbell was in his prime. It was as though it was just meant to be that year. When Karl came in, he got rid of 'bad eggs'. He looked at the situation and he said that he didn't want any dickheads in the team. He was very honest with the players and he had a great sense of humour. Even when he was telling you off, there was a laugh and a joke as well as the seriousness. He was laughing when the media were describing us as a team of misfits and when the TV crews came in the build-up to the final, he told us to be as normal as possible and not to get caught up in the hype.

Danny Maun

A very effective Chairman

Kevin (Nicholas) has been a good chairman for 25yrs. He's a bit like a father figure to me and he's done wonders for the club without wasting money. We used to manage without special training kit, without extra training gear. We didn't train in the gym and do weights until Karl came, but we were still able to beat teams that had more money.

Danny Maun

Batley is the best club I've played for and the type of club that it is, is one of the reasons why we were able to win the cup against a team that had more money and bigger names. Batley looks after you and your family. Kevin Nicholas doesn't like putting his hand in his pocket, but he will go the extra mile for the players and if the club had the money he would spend more.

The members of the team appreciated Kevin and knew that he was trying his best to help us out. Because he would go the extra mile for the players, we would do that for the club. 2010 was the highlight of my career. I was lucky enough to win it again in 2012 with Halifax but it didn't have the same feeling or enjoyment as 2010.
Sean Hesketh

It was such a good atmosphere

People didn't expect Batley to beat either Leigh or Widnes, but Batley are a team that gets the best out of players. It was a relaxed atmosphere and I could feel that as soon as I arrived at the club. We were mates/brothers and we would be together after the game. If we were behind by one try, we were all thinking that we can still win this game. Players were saying I'll defend for you and you defend for me. I played some of my best rugby at Batley because I was relaxed. The first game I played I had such energy because it was a good atmosphere.

We could beat teams that looked stronger than us because there was a great spirit amongst the team at Batley. There's a lot of tradition at Batley and the club cares about the players, like a family. Kevin Nicholas is great and that spirit has lasted. It was continued by John Kear and now Craig Lingard, who has seen how it works and is doing the same.

Alex Brown

A quiet confidence developed

We went through the group stages of the competition and we began to realise that we had a good team. We were underrated.

We didn't have any big names but we had players who were as good as any who were playing in the Championship. We weren't shouting about it, because we weren't that sort of team. We just got on with it and as we went through to the semi-final against Leigh we became more and more confident.

Even though Leigh were strong favourites to get to the final and probably to win it, we felt that we could beat them. It was just something that had gradually been developing in the team. It was a quiet confidence, something that is difficult to put your finger on, but the players just felt it. Of course, no one fancied us, but Karl had been telling us that we were going to win the Northern Rail Cup. Some people in the game might have laughed if they had known what he was saying, but we believed it.

Karl's team talks got shorter and shorter, because he knew what we could do.

Lee Greenwood

Quality players, no prima donnas and a special ingredient

In that season we had two half-backs who were on fire. Paul Handforth was experienced and he could run a game and orchestrate the team. Gareth Moore was just starting out, but he was quality and they were supported by players who were working their nuts off. There weren't any prima donnas in the team. Everybody had to muck in and if you didn't you wouldn't be accepted and you wouldn't be picked.

Batley had underrated players, so we were a better team than we were given credit for, but the team spirit gave us that extra bit. Some teams used to take the mickey out of Batley because of the sloping pitch. It was as though a club with a pitch like that couldn't have a serious team. It does come as a surprise to players who haven't played at the ground, but it's also part of Batley's identity and that feeds into the team. There was no place in the team for anybody whose ego was bigger than the team. The lads who were there, were there because they wanted to be part of the team. They were not there because they were getting loads of money and that helped to mould a solid team.

I'm not saying that we were all bosom buddies but we were certainly a group of mates. In that sense it was a bit like an amateur club, but with professional attitudes to playing the game. There was certainly something special about being part of that team and it was something that wouldn't necessarily be obvious to outside observers. It was an ingredient that they could easily miss and they often did, but it was one which made a big difference and shows why we were underestimated.

Everyone in the team would go to social events and it wasn't something they were forced to do. They wanted to be there. They weren't going to be fined if they didn't attend a social event, but they didn't want to miss out. There was a lot of banter and piss-taking and players knew that if they didn't turn up to these events they would have the piss taken out of them even more, but that was part of the team spirit.

Lee Greenwood

Players want to stay at Batley

We were able to win because of the attitude of the players and their desire to win and the belief that we could do it. A lot of that came from Karl Harrison, how he treated you and the way he spoke to you. Also, Batley had nothing to lose and Widnes had everything to lose because they were strong favourites. We were looked on as inferior and that spurred us on.

I think that the Batley team spirit is second to none. When players come to Batley from other clubs they always want to stay at Batley. The only reason they leave is if there are big problems commuting or they are offered a lot more money elsewhere. Players stay at Batley when other clubs are offering to pay them more. I think that the team spirit and camaraderie is what separates Batley from other clubs in the league. There's no room for big egos that can upset the team. Batley is run on a bare minimum, but it's that team spirit which enables them to do well. There is a community spirit at Batley, where they all help each other. There are all the volunteers who do things for nothing, like the women in the kitchen.

Mark Toohey

No cliques of players

The main reason we won, I think, is that we were a very cohesive team. The players I was playing with at Batley were not playing mainly for the money. They were not journeymen who were moving from one club to another in order to get some more money. Karl Harrison had selected them for what they could do for the team. They were not picked because they were a name, they had to fit in.

That meant that there was no room for egos, for individuals who thought that they were better than the rest of the players and that the team revolved around them. That's how Karl constructed the team and built confidence. There were not cliques of players. We were a whole team. There is a particular culture at Batley. It's a family club and I have really fond memories of my time there. The sort of atmosphere that existed made the players feel that they could achieve and that has continued to be the case.

Byron Smith

No sulking if you weren't picked

We were a solid team and there was a great togetherness amongst us, like a band of brothers. We were all prepared to work hard for each other and as the season went on our confidence and belief in what we could do grew.

It wasn't something that happened overnight. It was gradually built up and everything was sort of confirmed when we beat Leigh. By that time, we weren't bothered who we came up against. We just stuck together. The only people who were shocked was everyone else. We believed that we could do it.

That Batley team is the best group of people I've played with. There were no stars, just a bunch of young lads with a few experienced players like Tiger Handforth. He was able to lead the team and the players took notice of him. Though it wasn't a big squad, there was competition for the places, but there was no sulking if you weren't picked. That paid dividends because we operated as a team. Batley didn't have a lot of money, so the players had to want to play for the team because they could't be doing it for the money.

Sean Hesketh

We didn't let teams walk over us

I think that we were stronger as a team. We all got on and we worked for each other. There was also less pressure on us because we were clear underdogs. We felt that no matter what they threw at us we would be able to beat them.

Every member of the team made an important contribution. They all did something that would benefit the team and nobody gave up. We didn't let teams walk over us and when you have got that sort of atmosphere in a team, it's hard to beat.

I think that the team was easy to coach because all the players wanted to play for Batley. They wanted to win for the club and they knew how much it would mean to the fans because it had been so long since the club had won a major trophy.

Tommy Gallagher

Karl's approach was simple

Widnes had a really good team but that win against Leigh had given us a lot of confidence because we'd beaten them on their own ground and that gave us the belief that we could do the same against Widnes. Karl had no doubt that we could do it and when someone that big and that scary tells you, then you believe it. His approach was simple and that was that if everybody did their job and did the basics effectively, we could win.

John Gallagher

We bought into Karl's emphasis on defence

Widnes underestimated us. Maybe they thought that getting to the final was enough for us and that we'd just turn up and give it to them.

We were the underdogs and we had nothing to lose and we knew that it was just one man against another. We had beaten the favourites and that gave us loads of confidence. We had a fantastic team spirit. All the players got on with each other and there was loads of banter. Nobody was left out and we all grafted for each other.

All the players thought that it was a really good club to be at and they wanted to be able to win something for the fans. We also had some good players. Everybody bought into Karl's emphasis on defence and Tiger Handforth was a really good ball handler whilst Gareth Moore was an attacking player. Alex Brown was very strong and athletic.

Ash Lindsay

Although some players shut out the noise from the crowd, Paul Handforth has no doubt that Batley's fans had a hand in their team's victory.

The Batley fans were unbelievable

The Batley fans were unbelievable. They were real rugby fans who knew the game. They appreciated the effort that the players put in, even if we didn't win. They knew that we had tried. They really brought us home against Leigh in the semi-final and we were well aware of them during the final. They were great

Paul Handforth

It is unsurprising that Karl Harrison's role in developing a powerful team spirit within a very cohesive unit is top of the list of reasons that fans put forward to explain why Batley were able to defy the odds and win the Northern Rail Cup Final. The perspective from the terraces is best summed up by the following four contributions.

You could see the difference between Batley and Widnes

I think that one of the main reasons was the belief that the team got when they beat Leigh. Leigh had been hot favourites to win the Northern Rail Cup and although it was tough game Batley had dominated them at their ground. After that I think that the lads thought that they could beat any team in the Championship. They'd beaten the favourites so why not Widnes as well, even though Widnes hadn't been out of Super League all that long.

We had good players as well. Maybe not as many well-known names as teams like Widnes and Leigh, but underrated players. We had a team where they were all playing for each other and you could see that in the last few minutes of the game We had a team of local lads who had come up through the amateur game. It was great that someone like Mark Toohey, who'd played his heart out for the club, could be part of that victory. We had really hardworking players but in a way that doesn't fully do them justice because they were skilful as well. They weren't the best paid players, but that meant that they were at the club for more than just the money.

You could see the difference between Batley and Widnes. All the

Batley players believed that they could win together. Karl had got a team together, not just individuals. Those players wanted to win that cup for the club, not just for themselves. They knew how important it was for the community and they did it. I don't think that the Widnes players could believe it at the end of the game.

Malcolm Westerby (fan)

Batley had a very good side

Batley had a very good side. It contained some good players. Mick Govin, who only came on as a sub in the final was a very good player. The Gallagher brothers had been at the Leeds Academy; Johnny Campbell is still performing for Batley and there were the ball players, Gareth Moore and Paul Handforth.

Ash Lindsay would have been my first pick in a Batley team at the time. He was a top performer. It was also a local side with a lot of players hailing from no more than five miles from the ground and the vast majority, apart from Mick Govin, from no more than ten miles from the ground. There was a solid culture within the club and the team. All the players played for each other.

John Atkins (fan)

Widnes complacency

I think that Widnes were expecting to win and they got a little bit complacent, especially after they had gone into the lead. They should have known better because we had already drawn with them.

Barry Lee (fan)

More relaxed

I think that one of the main reasons was that they were not the favourites to win the trophy, so there was less pressure on them and therefore they were more relaxed.

Richard Drake (fan)

6.

THE FRONTIER
AND BEYOND

Celebrations – The Batley Calypso Club

We stayed in Blackpool after the game, but most Batley fans went back to the Frontier in Batley. It would have been great to go back there, but we had already made arrangements. It was pretty quiet in Blackpool on the Sunday night.

It had been much busier on Saturday night. We went to what we nicknamed the 'Batley Calypso Club' (because of all the singing before the match) and there were a couple of Widnes fans in there, so we completely 'tortured' them. They took it well, because it was all good-natured banter. We were in bars near the ground and we didn't have a particularly late night because the landlady at the hotel had said that it would be locked at 1:00am.

Back in Batley, it all kicked off at the Frontier when everybody got back there. A pity we weren't able to be there.

John McVeigh (fan)

Simply the best

We went back to Batley Nash because we thought that the plan was to celebrate there. Those who had gone by coach ended up at the Frontier. I think that was because the coaches left from and returned to the Frontier.

When we arrived back at the Nash, there were some people in the club who didn't know the result. Those who were in the games room had been watching it on the screen, so we were puzzled as to why the news hadn't been passed on. I suppose it was because the Sunday night crowd in the concert room had come for the music. Anyway, they were delighted when we told them that we had won. Some thought that we were having them on, but once it sank in they were delighted and ready for a booze-up. Not that they need an excuse for that in the Nash.

Anyway, in the Nash there was a turn on and we asked her if she could sing the Tina Turner song 'Simply the Best' and she said that she hadn't sung it before but she'd have a go. We all sang along with her and it was a great atmosphere.

Tony Grace (fan)

They relaxed the dress code

We had a really good night at the Frontier. It was so good I don't have any memory of what time we left the Frontier. They put on a special session because Batley had won the cup. The players came in with the cup and they went onto the stage. They arrived about an hour after the fans because they'd had to get showered and everything after the match. I think that they were given free drinks all evening or something like that. When they went up onto the stage there was loads of clapping, chanting and cheering.

What was different was that you were not normally allowed into the Frontier if you were wearing a rugby shirt. That breached the dress code, but this time because people had come straight from the match, they relaxed that rule. Well, they would have lost a lot of money if they hadn't relaxed the rule, because people would have gone somewhere else. Anyway, some of the bouncers at the Frontier worked at Batley's ground and some of them had been to the Final in Blackpool. Anyway, we had a great night at the Frontier. People were celebrating the win; they were singing, chanting and lots of people were talking about the match, reliving some of the key moments, especially that Alex Brown try in the last minute, which won us the match.

Luckily, I had booked the Monday off from work because I knew that I wouldn't want to be going in to work, especially if Batley had won. If I hadn't booked the day off, I would have had to phone in sick.

Richard Drake (fan)

Fairly quiet at first

When we got back to Batley we went to the Frontier. Eventually it was packed as the coaches arrived back from Blackpool.

On that evening it was just open for Batley fans. The coaches had set off from there, so it was very convenient when we all got back. Because we had been to Blackpool by car, we got back faster than the coaches, so it was fairly quiet in the Frontier when we went in but it soon started to get busy once the coaches came back. I didn't leave until 1:30am.

Peter Homer (fan)

Celebration at home

I didn't go back to the Frontier, but I had a fridge full of beer at home, so I was able to have a few drinks when I got back there. I got a recording of the match and I watched it a few days after the final.

Barry Lee (fan)

No charge to go in

We waited for the trophy to be presented and then we came straight back to the Frontier. We hadn't been back all that long when the players arrived. It was absolutely packed because there were the supporters who had been to the match and there might have been some who couldn't get to the game because they were working or had commitments, but they decided to come to the Frontier to celebrate once they heard that Batley had won.

There was no charge to go in the Frontier, but I imagine the owner knew that he was going to sell loads of beer and other drinks, so there would be a big profit on the night. I can't remember how long I stayed at the Frontier, but it was late when I left. I don't think that I had booked the day off, but I can't exactly remember. I think that I was probably on shift, so I wouldn't have been starting work on the Monday until later in the day.

John McGowan (fan and ex-player)

I had to return to Rugby the following morning

We went back to Batley on the coach and went to The Frontier. Everybody was elated and drinking and talking about the match and what a thrilling game it had been. It was like that on the coach as well. Everybody was buzzing and going through what had happened and how they couldn't believe how it had ended. This lasted till we got back to Batley and then continued in The Frontier. We didn't stay too late because I had to return to Rugby the following morning.

Stuart Merton (fan)

It was surreal

When the presentation was done, we drifted back to the coaches. I think that the instruction was that we should be back on the coach no later than half an hour after the game had finished. We bought cans to drink on the coach and once we got on, everyone was hyper. All the fans were talking about the match and particular incidents, but especially the last ten minutes.

It was surreal, like the whole thing was a dream, We had won a major trophy and this was the first major trophy in a long time. The whole coach was buzzing with talk about the match. The journey back to Batley seemed to pass by in a blur. When we got back, I think that I went straight home and got changed before going down to the Frontier for the celebrations. I knew that there was going to be something going on at the Frontier whether we won or lost.

It was about ninety minutes after I'd got there that the team arrived and then everything kicked off. It was fantastic, just a continuation of a great day. The majority of people who had been at the match went to the Frontier. There were probably some who went down there who hadn't been able to get to the game because they were working, so they came to the Frontier for the celebrations. I can't remember what time I left the Frontier, but it was late. I flagged down a taxi after I'd set off walking and he dropped me off and then dropped off the Huddersfield Town supporters who'd come to the Frontier with me. They thought that the whole day was brilliant.

Billy Lonergan (fan)

Pizzas and an open top bus parade

After we had cheered the players when they came out, we went back to the Frontier and the team arrived with the cup. A lot of us were hungry because we hadn't had anything to eat for quite a while, so they started cooking pizzas for us at the Frontier. It was pretty late when we left the Frontier, but as I was working for myself I wasn't worried about having to go to work the next morning because I hadn't arranged anything.

During the week there was an open top bus procession in the town which ended up at the market place. I was there with my banner and there was a news item on the local news.

Ged Littlewood (fan)

We didn't know about the Frontier

We came home after the match and I didn't have a drink after the game because I was driving. I had a few drinks when we got home but we didn't go to the Frontier because we didn't know about the celebrations there. If I had known, I might have gone along there but I wouldn't have stayed late because I was working the next day and I might have had to travel to Stoke or Halesowen.

Barry Dale (fan)

I couldn't have too much to drink

We went back home from the coach, but then I found out that people had gone to The Frontier, so I insisted that we should get a taxi to go down there. It was fantastic, because the players came along and people were taking selfies with them and there was lots of singing and cheering. It was a wonderful night, but because I was working the next day (as a Headteacher in a primary school), I couldn't have too much to drink.

Janet Virr (fan)

Walking up the middle of Healey Lane

I nearly missed the bus back to Batley because I have a brother who lives in Blackpool and I met up with him and we had something to eat and then I realised that the bus was leaving at about 7:00pm and I only just made it. Anyway, we went back to The Frontier and they had got it all ready for us. I was with Scotty (Mark Scott) and I can remember that the players brought the cup into The Frontier and they filled it up. It was a great night and we'd waited a long time for that. I can remember walking back home up the middle of Healey Lane between 1:30 and 2:00am. It was appropriate that Laurie Grailey, the club's historian, who died early the next year, had managed to see Batley win a trophy because he had hardly missed a match since he was a lad.

Malcolm Westerby (fan)

Restricted celebration

I was six months pregnant and I remember being gutted cause I couldn't get drunk to celebrate.

Leanne Allen (fan)

Shattered

I was in the army at the time. I drove home and went to the Frontier with my fiancée at the time and then dropped her home in Barnsley and then drove to Portsmouth for work; shattered, but so happy.

Daniel Hunter

Embarrassed wife

I am a Batley lad living in exile, so I got a return ticket from Wigan. Got a bit drunk and giddy. So it was one embarrassed wife and loads of bemused locals when she picked me up outside Wigan North Western, while I was waving my scarf and chanting "Who let the dogs out?"

Paul Smith (fan)

I held the trophy

Ended up at the Frontier and Paul Handforth gave me the trophy to hold while he went for a wee!

Paul Machon (fan)

Fans from both teams enjoying each other's company

We stayed at the ground for the presentation and then we went to various bars and pubs in Blackpool. There were quite a lot of fans who stayed in Blackpool for the Sunday evening. There were fans from both teams and I didn't witness any trouble, just fans from both teams enjoying each other's company.

A lot of Widnes fans would have booked to stay overnight in Blackpool and they wouldn't have cancelled that just because they had lost. In fact, they would probably have wanted to go out for a drink just as much as the Batley fans and the Widnes fans got on with them very well. Batley is a nice family club.

There is no history of Batley fans being violent towards the fans of other clubs. Batley is often the second favourite team of the fans from other clubs. A lot of clubs like to play at Batley. They like the hospitality and therefore they don't get too riled up if they get beaten by Batley.

Craig Lingard (fan and ex-player)

Suspicious mind

We set off back to Batley and we heard that there was a party at The Frontier, so we went there and it was a long night and an even longer morning because I had to be up early to get the newsagents ready for opening on the Monday morning.

Obviously the limo left us at the Frontier and I ended up getting a taxi home with Brendan Tingle. I'd had a bet on Batley to win at 7/2. I put £100 on, so I won £350. On the Monday, I was knackered, so my wife did most of the day in the shop after I'd opened up and got things running.

She encouraged me to go home and get some rest. I could barely walk upstairs and I ended up falling asleep on the bed fully clothed. Anyway, because my wife had looked after the shop for most of the day, I gave her £100 of my winnings and she said "What's going on? I don't trust you. You've never given me money like this before!"

John Atkins (fan)

I don't like being the centre of attention

We went back to the club after the presentation etc and we had a few beers there before we went to the Frontier for the big celebration. The players got their dancing/nightclub gear on. They got me to go up on stage at The Frontier, which I hadn't really wanted to do.

I'm a bit of a miserable bugger in those situations. It's because I'm shy really and I don't like being the centre of attention. I was with my wife and my parents, but I had to be at work next morning, so I wasn't able to have a really big session. The players were all texting me the next day about the great night that they'd had.

Karl Harrison

My kids had the next day off school

Back at The Frontier we had a great time. My kids were there, even though they were quite young. They had the day off school the next day because we stayed up till about 2:00am. I was certainly hung over the next day, but what a great time.

Paul Harrison (Chief Executive, Batley RLFC)

We sneaked in some players who hadn't been selected

After the match all the directors went upstairs to the boardroom at Bloomfield Road. I don't remember seeing any Widnes directors there, though some had been in there before the game. My son was very interested in going into the boardroom of a football club, especially as Blackpool were going into the Premier League at the start of the season. Ron Earnshaw was there and we managed to sneak in some members of the Batley squad who had not been picked for the match, so they could have a drink with us and the team. We knew that those who had not been selected would be feeling a bit disappointed, so that was the least we could do for them. We had a few photos taken and then we were ready to leave.

John Miller (Director, Batley RLFC)

I was the last to leave

When the coaches came to pick us up we loaded a few beers on board so that the lads could have a drink on the way back. The handle of the cup actually broke off the trophy as it was being carried off the bus, but I think it was mainly because it had already been damaged on a previous occasion and just stuck back on again. I think that we got back to the club for about nine o' clock and then we went down to the Frontier. The boys went up onto the stage back at the Frontier and it was absolutely nuts in there. Laurie Grailey was still alive then and he was at the Frontier.

I think that Tiger Handforth had the trophy most of the time we were in the Frontier. Someone said that Tiger Handforth took the cup home and slept with it. It was passed to Karl Harrison, but he said that he didn't want it and that he wanted the players to have it. I had been the first one in the Frontier and I was the last one to leave. We stayed as long as we could and I think that it was after 1:00 am when we left. As it was a Sunday it would normally have closed earlier, but they kept it open later because of Batley's victory.

John Miller (Director, Batley RLFC)

A great experience for my son

I had to go in to work the next morning and that was hard. It had been a brilliant day with some absolutely great memories. It was very special for me even though I sometimes feel guilty that if I hadn't joined the club as a director, perhaps we would have done more as a family, you know like visits to different places on Sundays instead of me being at matches.

On the other hand, Joe would not have had the experiences he had that day and that is something to savour. He was eleven years old and they were special experiences that none of his mates had. He was with the players before and after the match. He was exhausted by the end of it, but it was nice to share a day like that with him.

John Miller (Director, Batley RLFC)

I had to sign an indemnity

After the celebrations on the pitch, I was summoned by someone from the RFL and I had to go into this small room where I was asked to sign a document which was on a sheet of A4 paper. The document, which had my name at the top, was a declaration that I would take care of the Northern Rail trophy, for which I was responsible for the next twelve months.

I was signing an indemnity which made me responsible for any loss of or damage to the trophy whilst it was in Batley's possession. The document also contained a promise that I would return it to the

RFL twelve months later. I signed the document, but we hadn't yet received the trophy, though we knew in advance that the lid of the trophy did not come off. It must have been welded to the body of the trophy. Consequently, we had brought the Roy Powell trophy with us so that we could fill it with champagne, if we won the Cup. We had the Roy Powell trophy at the front of the coach.

Kevin Nicholas (Chairman, Batley RLFC)

The champagne drained onto the bus floor

After the players had showered etc, there were celebrations in the bar but we needed to get back to Batley because we were going to the Frontier.

Anyway, when I got on to the bus I asked where the trophy was and someone said that the players were bringing it to the bus. When it arrived, the handle had come off. I thought "well, that indemnity didn't last long!" I don't know whether that had happened before and it had already been weakened but we got it mended. I think that it cost about £80 to have it welded back on. I think that it was repaired by a local jeweller, but I can't remember which one.

You couldn't tell that the handle had come off once it had been reattached. The jeweller had done a good job. We couldn't fill it with champagne of course, so we used the Roy Powell trophy, but we didn't know that the Roy Powell trophy had a leak in the bottom, so the champagne just drained onto the bus floor. The players were trying to drink the champagne as quickly as they could, but it was a fairly big leak and we realised that there was no point refilling it.

Kevin Nicholas (Chairman, Batley RLFC)

Every player still had their medals on

We went for a breakfast on the Monday morning. Every player still had their medals on and they were like kings of Batley in Wetherspoons. We were all talking about the game and then we went up to the Commercial pub for Monday Club. After that it was back down to earth with training for the league games. Me and

Sammy(Haigh) took the cup to Skippers on Batley for the handle to be put back on. We phoned the rugby league to tell them and it came out when Leigh won it they broke it and they had glued the handle back on.

Jonathan Hooley (kitman, Batley RLFC)

Didn't get to bed for two days

It was crazy after the game. I saw the family, who were in the crowd. Kevin Nicholas was brilliant, the look on his face. For a change, he didn't have much to say, but his face said everything. The atmosphere in the dressing room was absolutely fantastic. If you could bottle that and sell that feeling, you'd soon be a millionaire.

We went back to The Frontier and I didn't get to bed for two days. We went on to Wakefield and we were still wearing the medals. All the family had been at the game and apart from my kids being born this was the proudest moment of my life.

Danny Maun

We went in through a side door

We had the presentation of the trophy and we celebrated in the dressing room and then we went back to the club and had a drink before we went down to The Frontier. We went in through a side door and straight onto the stage and I've never seen The Frontier rocking so much. It was unbelievable; absolutely fantastic. It was packed and the people were cheering and shouting. I'll never forget that; to be up on stage in front of all those people who were enjoying it so much.

Paul Handforth

My boss was very understanding

Of course, we ended up at The Frontier, which was packed, but the celebrations went on for a few days. I had told my boss that I wouldn't be in on the Monday, but then I rang him up and said that

The Heavy Woollen Victories

I wouldn't be in on Tuesday either. He was very understanding. On the Sunday at The Frontier, you could see how much that win meant to people. They'd been waiting a long time and it was great to be a part of that.

Kris Lythe

It's all a bit of a blur

At the end of the game, I was dragged off to do a random drugs test and then it's all a bit of a blur. I drank some champagne and we went back to The Frontier, but I don't really remember the details. I know that it was a good celebration because we were a group of lads who were not expected to win, but we did and we can look back on that.

Alex Brown

A buzz around the town

We went back to The Frontier and it was all set out for us. It was a fantastic night and especially because there were fans there who I'd seen at the club since I was signed at fifteen. It was a brilliant atmosphere and I'd made sure that I didn't have to go to work the next day. What was even better was that there was a massive buzz around the town for the rest of the season.

Mark Toohey

Tiger held on to the trophy

We had a great journey back to Batley on the bus, lots of celebrating and a marvellous atmosphere. We took the trophy into The Frontier and I think that Tiger (Handforth) carried it about and wouldn't let others hold it. He was so pleased to have captained the team.

We also did an open top bus tour in the town and lots of fans gathered by the Town Hall. It was fantastic to be part of all that, most especially because you could see that it meant so much to the fans. Batley isn't a big club and it doesn't have a lot of money, so this was a major achievement.

You could see it on the faces of the fans that they wanted to savour every minute of the celebrations.

Byron Smith

Several days on the 'pop'

It was wild. Once the presentation had been made, we went back to the changing rooms and we were there quite a while. We were having a good knees-up. There was a lot of singing and some dancing.

I think that Kevin had got some beer for us and it was quite a while before we went upstairs.

Kevin told us that he'd arranged a bit of a do for us at The Frontier and we had a great time there. I'd booked the Monday off work, but the celebrations went on into Tuesday, so that was a 'sick' day. It was well deserved and all the players were involved after the match. Nobody wanted to miss out.

We were all proud of what we'd achieved. Mick Govin, who'd joined the team in March and was from Leigh was just as much a part of it. Karl Harrison gave us a few days off training. He said that he didn't want to see us till Friday, so we had a good few days on the pop and visited a few towns.

Sean Hesketh

John dropped the trophy

When we got on the bus we had some beers and my brother, John, dropped the trophy and damaged the lid, which was typical. He'll probably say that it wasn't him!

The bus went up to the club and we had some beers there before we went down to The Frontier where there were family and fans. I think that we drank it dry.

Some of us went on to Leeds as well and some of us met up again on Monday and had some more beers. I fell asleep on the train and missed my stop. Dave Toothill, who lived in Oldham, had to come and pick me up and give me a lift.

Tommy Gallagher

It wasn't me

It was wild at the end of the game. I think that I picked up Gareth Moore and threw him over my head. I nearly broke his neck. There was a load of singing on the coach on the way back to Batley and we ended up on the stage at the Frontier. It was a messy night. We ended up at a nightclub in Leeds and we had the trophy.

I don't remember damaging the trophy before we got on the bus. I think it was Mauny.

John Gallagher

I gave my shirt away

We were all ecstatic in the changing room after the game. People were singing and dancing and even Karl Harrison joined in. Everybody had been patting us on the back and it was fantastic. We knew that we had won, but it was almost a state of disbelief. We knew that we deserved it and we had been hungry for it. We were all really pleased for Kevin because he's such a great bloke. He wasn't just the Chairman – anyone needing help, he would help them out.

After the game, I gave my shirt away to a kid who'd watched every game. I was really proud to have played for Batley.

Ash Lindsay

The Impact of Batley's victory

Fans and players are in agreement that Batley's victory in the Northern Rail Cup final substantially raised the profile of the club both amongst the pundits and other Championship clubs.

Subsequent to this victory, lowly Batley with its uniquely sloping pitch was recognised as a club that was able to punch above its weight, a fact borne out by the team's progression to the 'Million Pound' game in September 2022.

Richard Drake, a lifelong Batley fan, says "other clubs started to take notice of us and some were nervous about playing Batley, especially if it was in a knockout competition. Featherstone don't like to play us because they know that we can beat them."

The victory certainly boosted the team's confidence and Batley's raised profile may also have enabled the club to attract some players who might previously have given little thought to an approach from an apparently unfashionable club like Batley.

Batley's Chairman Kevin Nicholas, though, is less sure about this latter point: "This win gave the team more confidence, the idea that they had achieved something gave them a boost and the belief that they could achieve even more. It wasn't a question of us blowing other teams away, more a question of having a more confident set of players. It stopped players getting poached by other clubs as well. They wanted to stay at Batley. Obviously, if a club offered a lot more money to one of our players, it would be impossible for them to resist, but if it was just a little bit more, then they wanted to stick with Batley. I'm not sure that it enabled us to attract better quality players than in the past, but what is certainly the case is that once players come to Batley they want to stay at the club. That's why we've currently got a fair number of players who've been at the club a long time."

In addition to boosting the team's confidence, Batley's win also provided a massive fillip to the club's fans at a time when the country was about suffer a period of austerity which badly affected towns such as Batley. One has only to read the accounts of the fans' celebrations and the unalloyed joy they experienced, to recognise that this victory provided an escape from the gloom that was descending on many of them.

Karl Harrison's reputation as a coach was substantially enhanced by his successful Northern Rail Cup campaign, the consequence of which was an approach from Halifax, for whom Karl had played, an approach he was unable to resist. Nonetheless, Batley was able to replace Karl with the very experienced and successful coach John Kear, a feat which might not have been possible without Batley's enhanced reputation.

Since 2010, apart from one year, the club has been able to consolidate its position in the Championship, which is no mean feat given the highly competitive nature of this division. Since The Northern

Rail Cup victory, Batley has regularly finished in the top five of the Championship and, as indicated above, most recently contested the so-called Million Pound game against Leigh. Victory in the 2010 Northern Rail Cup final established the platform from which Batley has been able to build a successful outfit during the past twelve years.

Batley's victory, achieved with one of the lowest budgets in the Championship, perhaps sent a message to other clubs, as the Batley director, John Miller, suggests: "I think that Batley's win in 2010 showed other clubs what can be achieved on a limited budget. Our strategy is sustainable improvement and development. We don't spend money that we don't have. Obviously with covid and all the disruption, it has been particularly difficult recently but we are doing our best to manage our money sensibly."

The one thing that Batley's victory did not lead to was a permanent increase in Batley's average gate. As a fan, David Hopkin, says: "There is no doubt that the victory really rejuvenated local interest in the team and led to some people returning to the terraces, perhaps some who had fallen away when summer rugby started, which coincided with the formation of Super League and Batley being denied access to the top division. I don't mean to suggest that it led to a massive increase in crowds, because it didn't. It led to a surge of interest when Batley got into the final but those spectators didn't then start to attend home matches on a regular basis – doing the hard yards, not just the glory stuff."

The problem of low attendance is one for which the club has not yet found an answer, which is hardly surprising given that the main reason for the club's shrinking fan base is largely beyond its control. The demographic change which has taken place in the town, which now has a substantial British Asian population amongst which there is no tradition of rugby league, makes it particularly difficult for the club to expand its fan base.

On a more positive note, Jane Virr points out that Batley's victory helped the Batley Independent Supporter's Squadbuilder Association (BISSA): "BISSA benefitted from Batley's victory in 2010 because we were able to tap into the excitement it generated and produce some merchandise connected to the win. We hadn't been expecting anything like this, so we had to be quick off the mark once we had won. We ordered mugs and calendars etc and it made a noticeable difference to our sales that year. In fact, we still sell the occasional mug related to the 2010 Northern Rail Cup victory."

For the match referee, Robert Hicks, the weekend as a whole had a very specific impact: "On a personal level this was an important event because this was the weekend on which I met my future wife. In fact, I met her for the first time the night before the match. When it was the Northern Rail Cup final weekend, there used to be the Northern Rail Nines on the Saturday and Sunday. In 2010 they all took place on the Saturday and all the officials involved agreed to meet up for a drink. We met up in the Tower Lounge and Gary Tingle, who used to play for Batley, was there with a group of Batley fans, one of whom was Amy, who is now my wife. I met her again on the Sunday after the game and the rest as they say is history."

AFTERWORD

UNFORTUNATELY, BECAUSE I was retiring on 23rd July 2010, I could not spare the time for the return journey from Sheffield to Blackpool. Consequently, full of anticipation but maybe not quite believing that Batley could win, on 16th July 2010 I sat down to watch the spectacle on TV.

I acknowledged that Widnes were favourites to win, but I was pretty confident that Batley would put up a good fight. What I did not anticipate was the see-saw nature of the scoring nor the drama of Batley's winning try.

When Batley went into an early lead through tries by Walton and Hesketh, my initial nerves began to settle. However, no sooner had I got used to Batley getting the better of Widnes than the 'Chemics' started to hit their straps.

I was particularly concerned that the young Widnes halfback, Thackeray, might be able to wrest control of the match from Batley and start to give them the run-a-round. I was secretly hoping that Ash Lindsay would be able to clobber him (legally, of course) and put him out of the game. A tricky, feisty halfback can do some damage to the opposing side in the latter stages of the game, A prospect I did not particularly relish. Anyway, I was relieved that Batley were able to finish the first half three points ahead of Widnes.

During the interval, as the TV camera swept across the terraces and I could see how much the Batley fans, some of whose faces I immediately recognised, were enjoying themselves, I began to think that I had made a mistake in deciding not to drive over to Blackpool, but by then it was too late to do anything about it, so I drank a couple more bottles of Czech beer as a consolation.

During the second half, once Widnes took the lead I was beginning to think that they probably had too much firepower for Batley and would be experienced enough not to relinquish it.

I thought that Batley had the ability to win but would maybe need to pressurise Widnes into making some mistakes, and I was worried that as Batley's forwards began to tire, Thackeray would be able to take advantage by running at them.

As the match went into the last fifteen minutes, I had to answer a call of nature and just as I returned to the lounge Alex Brown was breaking through to score his first try.

After the successful conversion kick, which put Batley just three points behind Widnes, I was standing up and howling at the TV screen, exhorting Batley to score another try. As the minutes ticked away without another Batley score, I sank back into my seat, convinced that Batley were going to miss out.

No sooner had I resigned myself to a miserable evening than Batley got possession of the ball near the Widnes line, Gareth Moore measured his kick to perfection and Alex Brown outjumped the opposing winger in a magnificently athletic leap before twisting and getting the ball down over the try line.

I can't remember exactly what I was screaming and yelling, but suffice to say that it was replete with expletives. Fortunately, my wife was out in the garden and the neighbour in the adjoining semi was hard of hearing.

The advantage of seeing that final try on the TV was that it was immediately clear that Alex Brown had got the ball down cleanly.

Though Robert Hicks called on the services of the video referee, I had no doubt that the try would be awarded; the one advantage I had over my fellow Batley fans who were in the stadium. Had the try not been awarded, I can say with absolute certainty that we would have needed to buy a new television.

I'm sure the remaining two or three minutes of the match, after Gareth Moore had hit the post with his attempted conversion, were as tense for me as they were for the fans at Bloomfield Road.

Logically, with less than three minutes to go, Batley were in pole position but I could not block out of my mind all sorts of irrational scenarios in which Widnes would manage to pull off a spectacular try. In the end, Batley were able to play out the final two minutes close to the Widnes line and Batley had done it.

I went wild and it took me some time to calm down.

Eventually, it was only the realisation that I still had some administrative work to finish off before Monday which brought me down to earth. It was just as well that I hadn't driven up to Batley and gone to Blackpool on one of the coaches which set off from the Frontier, because I would have been unable to resist joining in with the celebrations when the coaches returned to that nightclub, the result of which would have been a few hours kip on someone's sofa before a drive back to Sheffield in order to get into my workplace by 7:30am.

John Roe (author and lifelong Batley fan)

APPENDIX 1

Dewsbury's path to the Championship Final in 1973

29th April 1973
Dewsbury 29 points v Oldham 14 points

1st May 1973
Featherstone 7 points v Dewsbury 26 points

6th May 1973
Warrington 7 points v Dewsbury 12 points

19th May 1973
Dewsbury 22 points v Leeds 13 points

APPENDIX 2

Batley's path to the Northern Rail Cup Final in 2010

7th February 2010
Batley 30 points v Widnes 30 points

10th February 2010
Whitehaven 26 points v Batley 34 points

14th February 2010
Batley 46 points v Swinton 10 points

17th March 2010
Gateshead 4 points v Batley 100 points

5th June 2010
Batley 26 points v Sheffield 16 points

17th June 2010
Leigh 4 points v Batley 25 points

18th July 2010
Batley 25 points v Widnes 24 points

ACKNOWLEDGEMENTS

A SPECIAL THANK YOU is owed to all those individuals who were willing to give up their time for interview. Also to my wife, Sue, who acted as my trusty scribe and to Scratching Shed Publishing for their usual support.

Appreciation is also due to the British Newspaper archive and to the following publications from which various items have been extracted: *The Batley News*, *The Dewsbury Reporter*, *The Huddersfield Examiner*, *League Express*, *The Liverpool Echo*, *The People*, *Pro-ball*, *The Spenborough Guardian*, *The Sunday Mirror* and *The Yorkshire Post*.

A special thanks also to Martin Flynn, Keith Mason, Bernard Shooman and Allison Simpson, who provided invaluable assistance regarding contact details for former Dewsbury players, and to John Atkins, Tony Grace and Darren Rhodes for the photographs they provided.

All photographs have been acknowledged wherever possible. If credit has not been obtained, it is entirely unintentional.

Investigate our other titles and
stay up to date with all our latest releases at
www.scratchingshedpublishing.co.uk